THE ART OF ELECTRONIC FUTURES TRADING

THE ART OF ELECTRONIC FUTURES TRADING

Building a Winning System by Avoiding Psychological Pitfalls

WILLIAM S. KAISER
JAMES E. GREEN

McGraw-Hill

New York San Francisco Washington, D.C. Auckland Bogotá
Caracas Lisbon London Madrid Mexico City Milan
Montreal New Delhi San Juan Singapore
Sydney Tokyo Toronto

Library of Congress Cataloging-in-Publication Data

Kaiser, William S.
   The art of electronic futures trading : building a winning system by avoiding psychological pitfalls / by William S. Kaiser and James E. Green
     p.   cm.
   ISBN 0-07-135585-5
   1. Electronic trading of securities. 2. Futures. I. Green, James Emerson, 1947- II. Title.

HG4515.95.K34   2000
332.64'5—dc21   00-055436

McGraw-Hill

*A Division of The **McGraw·Hill** Companies*

Copyright © 2001 by The McGraw-Hill Companies, Inc. All rights reserved. Printed in the United States of America. Except as permitted under the United States Copyright Act of 1976, no part of this publication may be reproduced or distributed in any form or by any means, or stored in a data base or retrieval system, without prior written permission of the publisher.

1 2 3 4 5 6 7 8 9 0 AGM/AGM 0 9 8 7 6 5 4 3 2 1 0

ISBN 0–07–135585-5

This book was set in New Aster per the BUS16 design by Pat Caruso and Paul Scozzari of the Hightstown McGraw-Hill Desktop Publishing Unit.

Printed and bound by Quebecor World/Martinsburg.

McGraw-Hill books are available at special discounts to use as premiums and sales promotions, or for use in corporate training programs. For more information, please write to the Director of Special Sales, Professional Publishing, McGraw-Hill, Two Penn Plaza, New York, NY 10121-2298. Or contact your local bookstore.

This publication is designed to provide accurate and authoritative information in regard to the subject matter covered. It is sold with the understanding that the publisher is not engaged in rendering legal, accounting or other professional service. If legal advice or other expert assistance is required, the services of a competent professional person should be sought.
—*From a Declaration of Principles Jointly Adopted by a Committee of the American Bar Association and a Committee of Publishers and Associations.*

This book is printed on recycled, acid-free paper containing a minimum of 50% recycled de-inked paper.

*This book is dedicated to my wife, Francine
(I don't know how you put up with me), my children
Justin, Matthew, Lauren, and Greg, my parents
and relatives, my business associates, and most of
all the "floor trader," the true entrepreneur, who took
the risks and laid the foundation that has created a
true "free marketplace."*

*William S. Kaiser
aka Zapman*

*This book is dedicated to everyone at ZAP Futures
for helping to make ZAP the success it has become.*

James E. Green

Contents

Foreword   xi
Acknowledgments   xiii
Introduction   xv

Chapter 1: History   1

Chapter 2: Current State of Electronics   19

Chapter 3: The Future of Electronics   25

Chapter 4: Setting Goals and Maintaining Discipline   33
Discipline   37

Chapter 5: The Psychological Indicators   39
Gambling and Impulsive Behavior   43
Fad or Speculative Bubble   44
Group or Mass Behavior   46
Media-Induced Opinions   48

Chapter 6: How to Choose the Right System   51
High-E Tendencies   56
High-E Approach for Success   57
High-I Tendencies   60
High-I Approach for Success   62
Even Tendencies   65

Chapter 7: A Five-Step Plan for Successful Electronic Trading   67
The Five-Step Plan   69

Chapter 8: The Core Indicators   75
Oscillators   76
Momentum Indicators   79

Stochastics   88
Relative Strength Index   97

Chapter 9: Moving Averages   103
Time Filters   108
Percentage Bands   108
High and Low Bands   108
Breakout Filters   109
Total-Range Filters   109
Percentage Filters   110
The Double-Crossover Method   110
The Triple-Crossover Method   111
Rubber Band Theory   116

Chapter 10: Volume and Open Interest   117
Volume   118
Open Interest   119
Interpreting Volume   122
Interpreting Open Interest   124
Commitment-of-Traders Report   126

Chapter 11: Defining Trending and Cyclical Markets   129
Determining Support and Resistance Levels   133
Money Management Techniques   134
Margin Requirements   136
Dollar Units   137
Contract Liquidity   138
Self-Discipline   139

The Voice of the Leaders in Futures and Electronic Trading   141
Interview with Glenn Susz   142
Interview with Charles Starnes   152
Interview with Patrick Catania   156
Interview with Donald Serpico   170
Interview with John Rand   176
Interview with Leo Melamed   183
Interview with Jack Sandner   194

Conclusion   205

Futures and Derivatives Exchanges   209

Glossary   225
Index   251

Foreword

If there's one constant in our lives as we begin a new century, it's the perception of the increased velocity of change. The way we learn, communicate, and even relate to each other has been revolutionized by changes in technology. In our business, the changes are epitomized in the revolution in financial markets spawned by the growth of a class of economically literate and technologically adept investors. These new investors are increasingly making the Internet their financial adviser—and are making the transition from being occasional market participants to truly becoming traders, teaming up with their computer to regularly engage in the challenge of the markets.

With all the changes taking place, however, there is still one thing that remains profoundly the same. Although traders may have more information, quicker access to the markets, and a broader array of programs and systems to choose from, the simple fact is that today's online traders, like the nonelectronic cohort that went before them, must know themselves well and possess the informed motivation to become competent at their task. And these traders must have the psychological capital to make it through the emotional peaks and valleys the market delivers every day.

Trading is a solitary act, and achieving a level of competency is a neverending pursuit. Having enough financial capital isn't enough. Being smart isn't enough. Having access to infor-mation isn't enough. To become competent at the discipline of trading requires a reserve of confidence and self-understanding that's tested with every click of "enter order."

Bill Kaiser and Jim Green have long been involved with individuals trading on their own and have been involved with electronic trading from the very beginning. They have seen the best and the worst of traders. In this book, they mine their experiences to offer insights about what online traders need to get started and to keep going. I think you'll find the results thoughtful and rewarding.

At Refco, we're dedicated to identifying opportunity for our customers and to providing the best-quality access to the markets. In keeping with our mission, we're happy to have Bill and Jim's ZAP Futures affiliated with the Refco Group.

Joe Murphy,
President, Refco, Inc.
Executive Vice-President and
Global Head of Futures, the Refco Group

Acknowledgments

When electronic trading was in its infancy, there were few supporters and legions of naysayers. Over time, perspectives changed and support grew. Electronic trading has become the mainstay of the futures business, and its growth is not in question. We would like to thank all those associated with our efforts at ZAP Futures. There is a long list of individuals who helped us introduce a new way of business to the marketplace and gave us welcomed insight into our efforts in this book, and we thank them all. Those to whom we owe a special debt of gratitude include Rick Gallwas, Charles Starnes, Glenn Susz, Steve Walsh, Joe Luchek, the Chicago Mercantile Exchange, Refco, Inc., Jack Sandner, Leo Melamed, Ellen Resniak, Jim Bertie, Susan O'Toole, *Futures* magazine, *Stock and Commodities* magazine, *Bridge Trader*, Joe Murphy, and, in particular, the man whose vision was the basis of it all, Steve Klemen.

The Art of Electronic Futures Trading

This book is about a powerful new technology that is reshaping our world and making sweeping changes in our lives, businesses, and the way we invest. It is about amazing new opportunities in the futures markets, and some of the responsibility that must go with it. What most of us don't realize is that the Internet not only will change how we invest, but will also fundamentally alter how we live and work.

We are at the beginning of a huge transition from an old economy to a new one and are facing such a massive change it is often hard to fathom. In this incredible era of radical new technologies that bring change and progress, we have new opportunities not only to achieve wealth, but also to manage our lives differently.

Gutenberg invented the printing press in the mid-1400s, a precursor to the information technology revolution. Then, 500 years later, in 1947, Bell Laboratories invented the transistor, which ushered in the beginning of a whole new technology and information age.

In the past, only brokerage firms and institutional traders had access to the research tools necessary to trade these markets. Today, however, information is available at your fingertips with the press of a button. You can search thousands of records in seconds and combine this information with technical evaluation, timing tools, portfolio management, and other forms of analysis. No doubt about it, the consumer reaps the benefits of this richer field of instant information and quick access to the markets, and with so little effort and expense.

The consumer manages the Internet. There are no CEOs or presidents to be found. The middleman has been cut out, and a direct producer-to-consumer distribution system has been set up with more products and services available at a lower cost. But by eliminating the middleman "broker," we've also eliminated a healthy synergy and an often-needed check on foolishness.

Successful trading requires more than high-speed electronics and systems. A hefty 95 percent of successful trading is due to psychological factors, and only 5 percent is due to the systems. Many people trade without a goal or plan and hope that the trades they make will be right. There is a twofold goal of this book. One is to introduce you to a systematic way to trade, and the other is to give you the psychological tools necessary to become a successful trader. Self-image and positive mental attitude help you avoid the frustrations and depressions that confront all traders every day. Greed and fear are the same whether dickering in a bazaar, bellowing across a trading floor, shouting into a telephone, or pounding wildly on a keyboard. Electronic trading isn't safer or less demanding emotionally; it is just quicker, cheaper, and easier to execute.

Using rational thought rather than emotions is the correct way to trade. Systems help take the emotions out of trading and mathematically define, quantify, and categorize past relationships in collective human behavior and give you a systematic probability for future behavior.

We have collected some of the tools for self-analysis and market analysis that should help the online trader gain the most from the trading experience, preserve sanity and equity, and acquire self-knowledge and a positive self-image.

We hope that you get a lot out of this book—in the end it's about you.

CHAPTER

1

History

Tucked away on the lower trading floor at the Chicago Mercantile Exchange (CME), juxtaposed to the High Tech Demonstration Center, sits a blackboard used to record bids and offers for the butter-and-egg market. This historical anachronism brings into sharp focus the dramatic change in communication that has swept all contract markets into the digital age, and stands as one testament to the history of the organized futures markets in the United States. Communications has always been the filament that made the markets possible. Standing today in the visitors gallery on the fourth floor of the CME looking across the trading pits below, you can feel the energy of the marketplace as traders erupt into bidding and offering in response to new "paper" (orders) in the pit. The air is punctuated with outstretched arms and cards being flipped from clerk to desk and from runner to clerk. All this activity is played out against the backdrop of walls of electronic tote boards, bringing to life in bright lights the price changes in multiple markets. Some of those trades, however, no longer result from open-outcry call and response, but from the keystrokes of traders whose bids and offers are matched within the low hum of the Globex2 system. No yelling, no flailing arms, no nodding confirmation that "we" have a trade; just the muffled clicks of keyboards as transactions are entered and data delivered.

The emergence of electronics to display bids, offers, and trades and the introduction of computers to manage the huge data flow through the exchanges are not the most profound ways in which electronics has changed the face of these markets. Price data from open-outcry bids, offers, and trades are now routed through a computer. Trades are cleared and funds cashiered with the stroke of a key. But most importantly, we also have traders from around the world operating from their desks through entirely electronic means without speaking to a broker or even having a trade executed on the floor. The ability to trade within the exchange through matched orders, combined with the potential for these systems to replace open outcry, has become the most contentious issue to face the futures exchanges in the last decade. The movement toward electronic trading appears to be inevitable. Just as the telegraph made it possible to communicate market prices great distances from the trading floors and the telephone made it possible for customers to deal with brokers in a timely manner, electronics will change the markets fundamentally and forever. The question is in what way and according to what timetable.

Before we gaze into the future, a brief look back to where we came from will help put these new markets and, perhaps, the virtual exchange into perspective. Many people associated with the futures business remember how it used to be and long for a return to that system. Some traders, still clinging to the questionable notions that open outcry will forever triumph and that they will always need open outcry for liquidity, talk about the early days of the exchanges as if exchanges began when these traders took their first jobs as "runners" for a neighbor or a family friend. Advocates of the time-tested open-outcry system of trading believe that no electronic system is as efficient as that which currently exists at the Chicago Board of Trade (CBOT) or CME. They argue that while there is a lot of conversation regarding electronic trading, most large customers are only concerned with their fill and don't care how the order was executed or who executed it.

The Chicago exchanges have a very rich and diverse history that, to a great extent, has helped give this city its rough and tumble character as the last frontier of capitalism. This is a proud tradition in Chicago, and for those who have spent their adult lives in the futures business, the new changes are not entirely welcomed.

There is no shortage of folklore surrounding the exchanges, their history, their legendary traders and characters, and the everyday camaraderie that makes the "floor" the noisy home to thousands of people for 8 stress-filled hours a day. How did the exchange come to be the institution it is today? Let us briefly trace the development of the electronics on the exchanges and look forward to where all this will lead us.

When trading could still be described as haggling, the simple act of meeting face-to-face and articulating as best one could the price for which one was willing to sell or willing to buy was instructive. It is out of this tradition of physical commodity trading that the exchanges grew. There are many colorful stories about the early characters involved in the commodity trading business, and each of them probably has some basis in truth. One of the most amusing stories about the early days characterizes the fundamental act of communication as the heart of a transaction. Bob Tamarkin, in his excellent and very readable history of the Chicago Mercantile Exchange; *The MERC*, tells the story of Max Weinberg, a German immigrant and charter member of the Chicago Mercantile Exchange when it was created in 1919. From very humble beginnings in the late nineteenth century, Max would go on to create Weinberg Brothers & Co., a trading company that became the oldest commodity firm owned by a single family. Max's lesson points out the necessity of being able to decipher what the guy on the other side of the trade is trying to convey.

It seems that Max was negotiating with another meat processor, and the language barrier that characterized the mercantile melting pot of the Water Street and Fulton Street markets finally got in the way of the trade. Max, in frustration, finally started flashing his fingers to indicate the price he would pay. The negotiations continued until Max lifted the other guy's offer by nodding yes when the other guy held up his right hand with all his fingers extended. Shortly thereafter Max and the processor met, and Max tendered what he believed to have been the trade price. The processor disagreed, and a heated argument ensued. The other guy held up his hand, and Max counted his fingers, all six of them. Max paid up. The moral of the story: Never assume anything in business. Although electronics has done away with the language barrier and has stripped away some of the wonder that once drove the markets, Max's lesson remains a touchstone for all traders.

As we mentioned, the blackboard was the focus of attention and would remain so for the first half of the twentieth century. Even before there were trading pits, the new floors at the exchanges were designed to be open and spacious areas that would give all participants a clear view of the boards. More recently, the design for a central bank of elevators in the middle of the trading floor at the newest CME (30 South Wacker Drive) was scrapped because it would take up too much space and reduce the line of sight.

Telegraphs eventually shared space with and then were replaced by telephones, and the age of electrified trading was upon us. At the CME on Franklin Street in 1928, the rules only permitted incoming calls, and there were no runners or clerks. Eventually, clerks and runners became commonplace (and have served ever since as the exchanges' farm team for new traders), and the role of the telephone broker became a critical link in opening up the markets to speculators and other market participants.

As late as 1968, the only things electronic at the Chicago Mercantile Exchange were the lights and the telephones. This was in the rather small exchange located at the northwest corner of Washington and Franklin Streets where the main items traded were pork bellies and cattle. Yet when this whole trading process was taking place, it was amazing how organized the apparent chaos was. The telephone would ring; a client would place an order; a clerk would take the order and give it to a runner to take to a broker in the pit. The broker would then bid or offer the order via open cry.

When the bid was hit or the offer lifted by another broker or local in the pit, these two traders and the exchange's price recorder would make a record. The two traders would record their transaction on trading cards: the buyer on the blue side of the trading card and the seller on the red side of the card. At or about the same time, the exchange's price recorder would list the trade on blackboards that covered the walls near the pit. Before the price recorder would erase the price history on a blackboard, he would take a Polaroid picture and place it in a scrapbook. The scrapbook comprised the official time and sales record.

This whole process of phoning in an order, running it into the pit, having a broker fill it, and recording it typically took less than 2 minutes. It was an efficient operation. To the casual observer it must have appeared truly amazing how fast clients and traders could lose or make money. Everything moved quickly, and an incredibly noisy exchange of information swirled around the pit most of the time. The atmosphere reeked of excitement and big business in a way most folks could never imagine.

As the exchange grew and the carnival kept getting bigger and bigger and moving faster and faster, the facilities and technology were rapidly becoming outdated. In September 1971, the Chicago Mercantile Exchange moved into a new building located on the northeast corner of Jackson Boulevard and Clinton Street, just across from Union Station. Remembering the first time he stood on the trading floor surrounded by other traders, Bill Kaiser recalls that it was massive and had electronic price recording boards mounted all over the two-story walls. The glitter of excitement permeated the atmosphere, and everyone stood in amazement in the middle of this new high-tech electronic trading floor. The same word came out of everyone's mouth—"Wow!"

For the most part, however, the process of moving the order from the client to the pit and back again did not change.

The high-tech electronic boards made the delivery of price information immediate, but the new technology had very little impact on the traditional method of order flow and execution. In fact, the new trading floor, because of its size, made it more difficult for runners to weave their way from the desk to the pit. Also, as the exchange grew, an ever-increasing number of brokers, clerks, runners, and local traders were flowing into and spilling out of the pits. The runners had to negotiate this human obstacle course every time an order was placed. As a result, the time it took to execute an order probably increased. The changes did not seem to bother anyone on the floor. The exchange was growing, and it was now a blinking panorama of wall-to-wall information.

In June 1972, President Nixon instituted price controls. Suddenly, the Chicago Mercantile Exchange and the Chicago Board of Trade were front-page news. Farmers and speculators both sold contracts of live cattle, hogs, pork bellies, and other commodities against the price ceilings established by the bureaucrats in Washington. Farmers and ranchers were cutting their herds by selling cattle at $68 to $70 in the cash market because of the price freeze while selling against that level in the futures market. From the producer's perspective, it made good business sense to sell all your cattle at the highest cash price available. Under the terms of the market jiggering set up by Washington, the futures market preserved the free market. Cattle were worth what people would pay for them. But because of the freeze, the cash prices were not going any higher.

As history has demonstrated time and again, what was logic in Washington was not always logical in the rest of the world, and Washington logic rarely translates into profits. (It rarely translates into logic.) The price freeze demonstrated that Washington's "econologistics" did not translate into anything good in the commodities markets. Cattle went up to $88 in the futures market, while the cash market hovered around the $70 level the government thought they should sell for. When central planning meets the free markets, the results are almost never good.

Farmers and speculators who sold cattle at $68 to $70 lost $18 to $20 per contract. The price controls represented a $2800 loss per futures contract. Virtually overnight, picketers sprang up around the Chicago Mercantile Exchange. The free markets had become the bad guys, and price discovery and risk transference were out the door. Transparency in the markets had been replaced by the smudged window against which every dissatisfied producer could press his nose in hopes of passing the blame to the pirates in Chicago. Despite everyone's intentions, the market is always right. The true market price had been discovered, and it was Chicago's fault. The pickets in front of the Chicago Mercantile Exchange protested the fact that the futures prices were higher than the price-control levels. Ultimately, exchange officials and the Feds jawboned the markets back on track, and life resumed its ordered chaos.

The vital role of the futures markets continued to grow, and new contracts continued to be developed. Principal among the new contracts were the currencies. These contracts revolutionized the way the world thought of money. As the role and importance of the Chicago Mercantile Exchange grew, its physical limitations also became more apparent. This mammoth, electrified trading floor was becoming ever-more crowded. Life at the Chicago Board of Trade was not much better. On both exchanges, only a finite number of yelling, pushing, pencil-jabbing traders, brokers, runners, and clerks could be crammed onto the floor.

The clearing firms needed additional telephone clerks and other support personnel on the trading floor to handle their increasing business. Floor space was at a premium, and so no additional expansion in personnel was possible. Since each clerk only had two ears and two hands and the floors were already overcrowded, the exchanges needed to devise a way to handle greater volume and an increasingly sophisticated and demanding client base.

In 1989, the CME and the CBOT pooled their efforts to develop an electronic order entry system. The resulting computerized order processing system was imaginatively called the Trade Order Processing System, or TOPS, and is used by all major U.S. exchanges. TOPS electronically sends information directly from the broker or phone clerk in an office to the floor, where all the relevant information to maintain an order book, advise the clearinghouse, and confirm the execution of the order to the customers has to flow. With TOPS this entire process can be accomplished within minutes or less.

Virtually overnight, the exchanges' order handling capacity increased exponentially without having to stack up clerks like woodpiles around the pits. Previously, real estate on the floors was like real estate in the suburbs: Location, location, location was critical. With TOPS, a clearing firm could expand its order desk "upstairs" in an office away from the trading floor and avoid having to hire new phone clerks and pay for additional costly phone equipment. TOPS is the standard order entry and fill reporting system. TOPS technology opened a window into the future that eventually will herald the end of open-outcry trading.

Using TOPS, a client would phone an order into a central order desk off the trading floor. The clerk would keypunch the order directly into TOPS, which routed the order to a printer on the trading floor near the firm's floor operations area. Runners would tear the order tickets directly from the printers and have them executed, endorsed, and on their way to the firm's back office in a matter of minutes. In a very short period most U.S. commodity exchanges adopted the TOPS technology. It was fast, and it reduced the number of errors in the order process.

As the number of commodity futures firms continued to expand their business, the inflation waves of the late 1970s and early 1980s provided the impetus for the advent of introducing brokers (IBs). Traditional clearing firms, called "futures commission merchants" (FCMs), sought to offer clearing arrangements to smaller, non-exchange member firms. Prior to the Commodity Futures Trading Commission's approval of the introducing broker category, clearing firms were required to open branch offices if they wanted to have a local presence. Because of membership requirements imposed by different exchanges, opening a branch office was an expensive proposition. With the approval of IBs, clearing firms could now have a local presence through quasi-branch offices. Instead of funding and supporting branch offices, introducing broker offices were owned and operated by entrepreneurs, who usually provided the finances and the personnel necessary for the day-to-day operations. These far-flung offices introduced and cleared their clients' orders through the clearing firms. It was not long before a network of introducing brokers sprang up throughout the country. If necessity is the mother of invention, this network of introducing brokers brought with them Mom's worst nightmare—how to provide efficient and fast service to all these kids.

Linnco Futures Group was one of the early players in the IB business. Linnco had hundreds of IB offices, mostly in remote locations. Steve Klemen, the owner of Linnco, believed that the future of the IB business was inextricably linked to technology. He provided the impetus and the capital for the next step in the development of publicly available trading technology. Linnco's IB offices shared a common technology link. Most of them were connected to the home office through Linnco's satellite communication system. This satellite system enabled IB offices to receive preliminary reports of customer activity, final equity runs, research, live audio squawk box, monthly statements, and more.

In 1992 Linnco took the next step in implementing technology in order to bring its level of service one step closer to cyberservice. Linnco designed a DOS-based software program called Linnco's Electronic Order Entry System (LEO). This one-way dial-up program made it possible for an IB to transmit a customer order directly from its remote office to Linnco through the satellite system. In 1994 LEO was linked to interface with the exchanges' TOPS computers. Both the IB and Linnco could save time, process more orders, and reduce costly errors in moving orders from the IB to the trading floor. Linnco was able to reduce the size of its main order desk, while the IB was able to transmit orders from a PC and receive confirmation that the order had been received.

The next logical step in the implementation of electronic order entry was to expand the availability of LEO and offer it to the retail public. If IBs could enter orders over the satellite, why shouldn't the individual trader in New York or San Francisco be able to? There was reluctance to give the public access, which can be summed up in a word, risk. In 1994 when the ZAP Futures Division of Linnco (by that time renamed LFG) first introduced electronic order entry to the public via this satellite system, risk was the major concern. Other than the customer, who on the business side was going to assume the risk if something went sour with the satellite system or a computer? In the futures business, whoever takes the reward also takes the risk. As principals in the ZAP Futures Division, we decided to take that risk and almost immediately we felt the sting of arrows in our backs from naysayers. What could go wrong did go wrong.

For the average person, LEO was cumbersome and required expensive equipment. It was not surprising that in its first year of public availability, only one system was sold. In late 1995 LFG released a modem-to-modem version of LEO. A link from a telephone modem on a trader's computer could now give him direct access to TOPS. This modem-to-modem delivery had its problems, however. Modem technology in 1995 was not very sophisticated, and making a connection to another modem depended not only on modem speed but also on compatibility. It sometimes took 20 to 30 seconds for the modems to connect. This delayed connection was acceptable for longer-term overnight traders who did not require the immediate order confirmation a day trader demanded. Another problem with modem-to-modem communication was that after an order was transmitted, the modem would disconnect. Thus, LFG was unable to transmit the fill price back to the trader and had to rely on a traditional telephone callback.

The fill reporting "problem" was not really a problem in the early versions of the modem-to-modem system since the system was not designed to deliver fills, only to transmit orders. But this inability to deliver fills quickly became a problem and continued to plague the programmers at LFG until one day Bill Kaiser recommended that fills be sent to customers via the fax program inside their computer. When the fill came back over TOPS, it would be immediately transmitted to the client, who would program his fax program to show the fill on his screen. It was not an elegant solution to the fill problem, but it was the only way to get the fill back at that time, and the whole process from point of transmission until the fill was received could take anywhere from 3 to 7 minutes—a far cry from the 3 to 5 seconds that we see today. However, the order was received in 3 to 4 seconds from the point of transmission, and it was filled in a timely manner, usually under 30 seconds. In meetings we spoke about the fact that electronically transmitted orders were filled in about half the time of a traditional order phoned in to an order desk.

There was, however, an educational void out there among the trading public on using electronic order entry, and the LEO software was not exactly flying off the shelves even though we gave it away. The gaping delay in our ability to get the fill back had created the illusion that the entire electronic order process was slower than the traditional method of phone orders. We realized that educating the public on how the system worked would take time. The answer to what the consumer really wanted, greater speed, more power, and a truly integrated two-way system, lay in the power of the Internet. Thus in 1996, the Internet became the focal point for new development. As we learned more, we discovered that the Internet would give us the ability to provide instant communications at an extremely low cost with very dependable results. Unfortunately, this was at a time when the Internet was not the revolutionary medium it has become, and most people approached it with skepticism and distrust.

Aside from the government and teenagers in chat rooms on AOL, colleges seemed to be the only other group using the Internet. In late 1996, ZAP Futures began marketing the first Internet version of LEO to the public under the trademark name ZAP. It was the first time that the futures trading public could send an order to the floor from virtually anywhere in the world and receive a fill through the Internet. An order transmitted via the Internet would hit the trading floor in 2 to 3 seconds, it could be filled in the trading pit in another 10 to 12 seconds, and the fill would be returned to the client in an additional 5 to 10 seconds. It was now possible to use the Internet to send an order and receive a fill in 20 to 30 seconds without ever having to talk to a clerk, get a busy signal, or get put on hold. Commodity traders everywhere embraced it, especially those who were already using computers for most of their analytic studies. The ZAP high-speed online order entry system was about to become the standard in the industry.

The Internet was changing the world in ways never imagined, and these changes, even if in perception, were starting to wreak havoc in the protected world of exchanges. Direct electronic trading had been available to exchange members through Globex, Project A, and Access for some time. As long as the members of the exchange were the gatekeepers and controlled electronic trading, electronics were OK. Customers did not have direct access, and electronic trading took place after regular trading hours. But things were changing, and as discussed later, not all the electronic change was welcomed.

In all the industry magazines and at all the trade shows, electronic trading was the topic of conversation. Some of the products offered by firms were actually order entry by fax, and yet they too were being marketed as "electronic." Everyone wanted electronics so much that some firms marketed systems that existed only as "vaporware." They would be available soon. So although true electronic order entry via ZAP and electronic computer-to-computer trading through Globex were slowly gaining ground, the possibilities for electronic trading were only slowly gaining broad public acceptance and were being resisted by the members of many exchanges as a threat to their function as gatekeepers of their edge as pit traders.

Understanding that electronic order entry was not going away and in an effort to facilitate order flow into the markets, the Chicago Mercantile Exchange introduced its Universal Broker Station (CUBS) to the S&P pit in May 1997. The CUBS unit is a pedestal-mounted laptop computer that was placed directly in the S&P pit so orders could go directly to the broker in the pit rather than be run in by a runner or flashed in by a clerk. The broker would receive the order in 2 to 3 seconds, and the computer would organized the orders according to market price. LFG was the first clearing firm to have a CUBS unit in the S&P pit and once again took the lead in advancing technology. ZAP electronic order entry coupled with access to a CUBS unit became the techno-combination that all retail firms wished they had. We suspect that these firms were also glad to let LFG have all the problems, because as with all innovations, there were delays, programming issues, and connection hitches, and frustration was in great supply. Eventually, after a great effort by the CME, the problems with the CUBS unit were resolved and direct order into the pit grabbed the public's attention.

In September 1997 the CME again took a highly innovative step and provided a link between its Globex computers and TOPS. The Globex system had been primarily used for overnight trading and allowed brokerage firms to trade around the clock. The vast majority of retail traders, however, continued to trade only during the daylight trading session. In the Globex system for S&P's transactions, the computer matched bids and offers. There were no brokers and no local traders providing liquidity. It worked this way: London trader A made a bid or offer, and it was matched against New York trader B's offer or bid. When the orders matched, the trade was complete, all within the computer. The CME was truly about to open its trading facility to the general trading public, and by doing so it was taking a step from which it could not retreat. The act of opening its facilities to the public would change permanently the role of the membership and the perception of the exchange.

The first contract to be traded on the newly opened Globex platform was the E-mini S&P. The E-mini was so called because it was electronic and the contract size was one-fifth the size of the standard S&P. As all new contracts go, the volume and interest in the E-mini S&P began slowly. In just a few short months, however, the volume and point spreads were very respectable. The E-mini contract was unique in that in addition to allowing computer-to-computer trading directly by the public, it also offered local traders an opportunity to get involved. Trading desks with computers were located next to the open-outcry pit, and this allowed local traders an arbitrage opportunity between these two fungible contracts. If the E-mini S&P market was trading higher or lower than the S&P open-outcry market, the locals could buy or sell the two different contracts and make the spread difference between them. This arbitrage added volume to both contracts and gave the locals on the floor an opportunity to scalp the markets. This opportunity was also open to public traders since they could also trade both markets. You needed five E-mini contracts for every full-size S&P traded, but assuming you bought or sold five E-minis and did the opposite with one full-size S&P contract, you had no market risk. In terms of acceptance and volume, the E-mini S&P is one of the most successful contracts the CME has ever offered. The CME has since made available more than a dozen electronic contracts, and surely more will follow.

CHAPTER

2

Current State of Electronics

A ny discussion of electronic trading at the biggest boys club in America has to include its history and current politics. After all, it was open outcry, the free-market system at its finest, freest, and fiercest, that built these exchanges. Open outcry is the very foundation on which the commodities markets exist today. The momentum toward electronic trading was initiated by European exchanges that have enhanced electronic trading platforms. Ironically, the Globex model that was available to European traders during their work hours helped inspire the shift to an electronic trading platform. The MATIF, the French futures exchange, was one of the early adopters of Globex, and its members constituted a large portion of trading volume. After the MATIF was purchased by Société des Bourse Français (SBF), there was a strong motivation to improve technological capabilities.

The February 1999 agreement between the CME, the SBF, and the Singapore International Monetary Exchange (SIMEX) established a common trading platform for futures and options that is open almost continuously over the Asian, European, and U.S. trading periods.

Recently the SBF (including its two subsidiaries, MATIF SA and MONEP SA) announced the first global alliance with the CME and SIMEX that permits the individual trader to direct and execute trades almost around the clock with exchanges in Paris, London, Montreal, São Paulo, Singapore, and, of course, Chicago.

Additionally, the CME's Financial Industry Exchange (FIX) will allow brokers to link their front-end systems directly with the exchanges' systems, giving qualified customers the ability to trade, 24 hours a day, from their home computer. In addition to having a common trading engine that is accessible from a single terminal, the alliance provides for a mutual offset system (MOS) that allows members to establish positions on one exchange and offset them with subsequent trades on another.

Exchanges such as the MATIF and the LIFFE have closed their open-outcry pits, and others, like the DAX, have always been electronic. The growth of European exchanges has increased the pressure on U.S. exchanges to speed up the pace of electronic development. The threat to the open-outcry system caused by the advent of electronic trading has created a maelstrom in Chicago and New York. Electronic trading directly threatens the historic role and power of the membership. In addition to conferring membership privileges on their owners, memberships are bought and sold as investments. Membership seats form the basis of many traders' net worth, and that net worth is under attack from around the world.

In 1998, CME seat prices fell from a high of $695,000 in March to a low of $180,000 in September. In March 2000, as the new electronic systems took hold, there was a rebound, and seats traded at $750,000. However, falling seat prices put financial and psychological pressure on all members of the exchanges. Many traders leveraged their seats and borrowed against the equity. Moreover, many traders financed the cost of their membership. In a typical transaction, if you purchased a seat when the price was $600,000, you generally borrowed half the cost, or $300,000. When seat prices fell below $300,000, banks required the members to refinance their seat at the new rate, again putting half of the $300,000, or $150,000, in cash. The collapse in seat prices forced many banks to sell the memberships, which added to the already depressed seat prices.

The revaluation of membership prices was not the only change affecting the exchanges. Exchange members are mixed on the impact of electronic trading and what it means to their future, although the meaning is becoming clearer every day. At this point members are divided on many issues and have not determined how to benefit from this new wave of interest. The Chicago Board of Trade in February 1999 voted that open outcry was the way of the future by ousting Chairman Pat Arbor in favor of David Brennen, whose platform was open outcry. To the outside world it was if the members were trying to will open outcry back into its place of prominence. Since then, the CBOT reversed itself and has taken steps to ally itself with Eurex in an effort to take advantage of electronic trading.

Much of the pressure pushing the CBOT to embrace the new world of electronic trading has come from the development of a new exchange whose immediate reason for being is to challenge the CBOT's leading financial contract, the U.S. Treasury bond contract. In the spring of 1999, Cantor Fitzgerald, the world's largest 30-year cash T-bond broker, received approval from the CFTC to operate as a futures exchange. This new exchange grew out of an alliance between Cantor Fitzgerald and the New York Cotton Exchange. Historically, Cantor Fitzgerald was an institutional dealer. However, its strategic alliance with the newly renamed New York Board of Trade is threatening to take volume from the CBOT. The notion that any single exchange has all the power it needs to control its future is now a distant memory.

In June 1999, on the other side of town, the Chicago Mercantile Exchange opened its second electronic contract, the E-mini NASDAQ, and in October 1999 began offering the E-mini Euro and the E-mini yen. The CME's Globex2 system became operational in January 1999 and is capable of processing 10,000 trades per minute. This is three times faster than the system it replaced. The CME also holds licensing rights to both these products and should not see competition with those trademarks until 2010. The CME is currently adding some agricultural contracts to the E-mini series.

Like all systems, advances in technology are going to make today's systems look like blackboards in 2 years. Currently, most orders are being transmitted electronically but are being filled via open outcry. The only contracts that can be traded 100 percent electronically from a PC are the CME's Globex2 products. In June 2000 ZAP Futures gave individual traders the ability to trade all Globex2 products 24 hours a day.

One way that the exchanges make money from the computers is to offer side-by-side trading. Computer terminals are placed surrounding the trading pits where local traders trade the computer prices against the open-outcry market. For example, if the T-bonds are trading at 120.11 in the pit and 120.13 in the computer, a broker on the floor with a terminal mounted next to the pit could buy at 120.11 in the pit and sell simultaneously at 120.13 on the computer. The advantage is obvious since the floor trader sees both trades at once because of his or her physical location and is able to scalp 2 ticks, or $62.50, per contract, out of the market. Currently, side-by-side trading is being conducted at the CME in the E-mini S&P 500, E-mini NASDAQ, and the Eurodollar. The CBOT offers side-by-side trading in the 30-year T-bond. This is a positive situation for both the open-outcry pit and the computerized Project A in that it adds volume to both pits and gives the broker a new opportunity to make money where none existed before.

TOPS, developed by the CBOT and CME, is the electronic order entry system that most brokerage firms use to send orders from their order desks to the appropriate trading pit. Many firms have developed computer interfaces that allow clients to send orders from their PCs directly into TOPS. When the order is routed through TOPS, the client receives a time stamp and order number from the actual exchange for accurate record keeping. Other companies have developed proprietary order routing systems where orders are routed through the Internet and then directly to the broker in the pit via FM signals. The pit broker is holding an FM receiving unit to receive the order. Once the order is received and filled, the pit broker endorses the order and sends it back the same way.

By sending an order directly into the broker's hands, you are eliminating the necessity for the traditional phone clerk and in most cases an arbitrage clerk to hand-signal the order into the pit. The handheld units, whether they are the exchange's CUBS or electronic clerk (EC) units or privately developed units, also act as an organizing deck for the broker. As orders come in, they are placed in the "deck" in the order that they should be filled. Buy orders are arranged from high price to low price so that as the market falls, buy orders are uncovered as the prices are reached. For example, if the S&P market fell 500 points in less than a minute, 500 points' worth of buy orders would show up on the broker's screen as one order with the proper total quantity. A traditional broker who fills his or her orders from the traditional slips of paper would have to count the total number of contracts that need to be filled. After that, if the market is at a different price, there is the possibility that the quantity to be traded is wrong. By contrast, floor brokers with the computerized trading decks see the prices in the market change and the quantity that they see on their unit is also changing. This method of filling orders is more efficient for the brokers and gives the clients a much better chance of getting their orders filled.

Several proprietary trading systems have been developed by firms as a means of accelerating the use of electronics. These firms have developed a screen-based order routing system that utilizes a high-speed communications network tying together the trading desk with floor brokers. Orders are electronically routed to traditional open-outcry trading pits where the executing broker has a wireless handheld computer. The computer maintains up-to-the-second market information that traders can access directly. Orders are instantly communicated to these computers and are executed with fills confirmed in a matter of seconds. The system holds all the trading information, and no paper is generated.

3

The Future of Electronics

When people discuss the ongoing changes in the futures industry, the tenor of the conversation is usually motivated by the relationship each participant has to the industry. Neither the trader, nor the member, nor the regulator is immune from change (even though they may all be reluctant to embrace it), and all are trying to adapt to a rapidly changing future. Change is OK, each says, as long as it does not affect me in a negative way. Sometimes the process of accepting change is a seamless melding of ideas and interests. In the futures arena, however, competing efforts to adapt to change may resemble the efforts of two cats tied together and hung over a clothesline. Independence, ego, and a scramble to get the edge have never been in short supply. In order to look into the future and discern whether and how these pieces will fit together for the retail trader, it is necessary to view the change from the perspective of each.

The trader we are referring to in this context is not the large institution. Our focus is on the retail trader, regardless of size. Some would argue that there is no place for the retail trader in the futures market and rely on the premise that the institutional trader is the only entity suited for such a risk-filled venture. Regardless of the justifications, the retail trading side of the business is growing, so those arguments should fall on deaf ears. As more individuals trade equities, for the short term or even day trading, a continual flow of new traders enter the fray every day. Moreover, the retail public has shown a remarkable willingness and ability to embrace new trading technology. Not much seems to faze these traders or deter them. The appeal of the last frontier of capitalism is lasting whether the borders of the frontier are bounded by the open-outcry pit or computerized trade matching. So where is their future?

If we disregard the "futuristic" connotation of the future, i.e., trading chips embedded in our heads so we can "think" a trade and "will" it to be executed, the real quantum leap can be traced from telephoning a broker to trade to the fully integrated trading platforms that allow traders to manage portfolios, obtain quotes, and enter orders. The reality of the fully integrated automatic trading platform is already here. Over the next few years the innovations and enhancements to technology applicable to trading will be eye-popping. But even now, the combinations of technology and services associated with that technology have made the retail trader virtually independent.

Consider this. Traders can operate from a single platform, and through that platform they can manage multiple portfolios in multiple markets, test trading ideas, program systems directly into their computers, have access to a full panoply of analytic studies, receive quotes, and execute orders. New technology may make these functions smoother and faster and probably combine some of the activities, but the essentials are in place. If pushing a button to trade is the objective for hands-free trading, then the future is here. Traders now have the ability to program their system or methodology directly into a platform so that trading signals will be generated when a specific price is fed into the system from a quote feed. Orders are automatically created from the signals and placed into a pending file in the ZAP order entry software. The trader can review the order and transmit it for execution, or for those brave souls, it is possible for the orders to be written and transmitted automatically without the trader reviewing the order. For each step in the process an audit trail is created and written to a file for later retrieval. Not bad. But is it good enough?

Technology for technology's sake is not going to be an effective additive for traders. Useless bells and whistles may serve only to delay trading and to confuse the user. Even now some of the technology and programs available verge on overkill. As the applied potential for technology outpaces other areas of the trading business, there will be an ongoing sense of waiting for the rest of the world to catch up. This is not a new phenomenon. Ask any brokerage firm that is required to mail daily statements to the same clients to whom it transmits the very same data electronically. Timing may be everything, but it depends on whose time you are using. Thus, technology must still fit within a system that can accommodate it until such time that the system is plugged into the future.

One problem with plugging into the future is the uncertainty of what the future is going to look like. Accompanying that problem is the escalating challenge of who is going to shape the future and to whose specifications is it going to conform. Although technology is only one aspect of this challenge, it is a very big aspect. One result of new technology driving the future is the structural change taking place in the operational end of the business. It is in this arena, control over the means of production, that the heart and soul of the business end of the industry is being redefined. Adding to this debate is a constant litany of questions: What role will the exchanges play in the future of trading? Are they necessary? Who will regulate the industry? How far can market integration go before it becomes one market? What roles will the large institutional houses and banks assume in the new order of things? Although the public is conspicuous by its absence from these debates, its position in the scheme of things will be altered. That much is for sure.

It seems that not a day goes by that there is not a new story circulating about the divisive debates going on inside the exchanges. And rightly so. Technology has put the future of all exchanges into play, and they are scrambling, in their own ways, to ensure that they remain vital and, most importantly, necessary institutions. The exchanges are finally realizing that if they do not "eat themselves" by setting up relationships with electronic exchanges while continuing open outcry, they will be eaten by those exchanges.

The traditional roles of the exchanges have been to provide execution, clearing, and settlement of trades by members for and on behalf of themselves and the public and, further, to provide such services within a regulatory framework overseen by the federal regulatory agencies. Performing these services will continue regardless of the technology employed to perform them or the framework in which they are performed.

The conclusion that is often wrongly drawn from the shifting fortunes of the brokers and traders on the floor of the exchange as an institution is that closing the floors means that the exchanges will disappear. The exchanges will not disappear. They will most certainly change, but they will, by necessity, exist. This assumption avoids the last-refuge argument that "they" can't close the floors because of what it would do to liquidity. The bids and offers would have a wider spread resulting in a larger point or cash slippage. Even though the European experience with liquidity may be different, the character of the markets is such that the common denominator of efficiency, as directed by technology, dictates their demise. The most efficient marketplace will attract the greatest number of traders.

This statement, however, poses yet another scenario for the future of retail trading: The possibility exists for a bifurcated market in which institutional participants (usually exchange members) would trade on one exchange or in one division of an exchange and the retail public would trade in a separate arena.

Numerous arguments support such a bifurcated market. The large clearing firms and institutions ask why they should have to pay more to execute and clear within the framework of an institution that is not sensitive to their needs when they have the capital to create their own exchange. Such a scenario could leave the retail traders to trade on an exchange where the transactional costs were greater in proportion to their volume. The limits of loyalty to a way of doing business are often tested by the bottom line. If such a structure were innovated into existence, the exchange might still be able to capture the clearing side of the order flow, but not every step of the trade. Of course there are issues of liquidity, fairness, and economic purpose that would have to be addressed before such a scenario could ever come about. Other alternatives include the development of electronic communications networks (ECNs) similar to those currently operating in the equities markets. These ECNs may be developed independently or be a network of major institutions, users, or retail brokerages.

From the regulatory perspective, any changes in the structure of the market, say a bifurcated market, would face intense regulatory scrutiny. That is not to say, however, that such a market structure would not be approved, all other issues being resolved. As in the equities where orders may be routed to a regional exchange on which the desired stock also trades, having multiple markets for similar futures contracts is not unknown (COMEX gold and CBOT gold or the Mid America and the CBOT). Still, the separation of the marketplace into a "professionals" or "institutional" marketplace and a garden-variety "retail" market would be a more difficult structure for regulators to buy. However, as technology and economics continue to converge on the efficiencies of scale, separate markets could develop. Since the greatest percentage of the volume on the contract markets is derived from institutional traders, it is not inconceivable that the Commodity Futures Trading Commission (CFTC) would approve a separate market tier for institutional traders. Thus, to think that the market structure will continue as it is today is to miss the possibility that a tiered market could arise.

Nothing will happen to the market structure without the approval of the federal regulatory agency charged with oversight of the futures market, the CFTC. Regulatory oversight is one of the functions that has been traditionally performed by the CFTC, and for non-exchange members, by the National

Futures Association (NFA). This structure is unlikely to change, although there may be a "super" regulatory agency charged with oversight of all financial markets. As far as the retail trader is concerned, the customer protections in place are not likely to be lessened; and in view of the increasing globalization of the markets, it is more likely that such protections will be increased and extended to protect the trader who is trading on markets regardless of their location.

One of the biggest changes to face the retail customer will be the means of communicating with a broker and sources of up-to-date information now accessible using Internet-capable cellular telephones. Customers can use their wireless phones to place trades, check positions, and access real-time quotes. Other systems are being developed by various brokers in data providers using personal data assistants (PDAs) that can receive and transmit data. Some of these systems are based on the Palm PDA operating system (OS); others use systems operating on Windows CE OS.

CHAPTER 4

Setting Goals and Maintaining Discipline

The famous retailer J.C. Penney once said, "Give me a stock clerk with a goal and I will give you a man who will make history. Give me a man without a goal and I will give you a stock clerk." Goals are the invisible driving force behind our need to achieve. Many people undertake a project with good intentions and then fall flat or short because of poor or zero goal planning. Although many positive things can be said about goals, some of their most powerful benefits are that they help you focus your energies on the job at hand and allow you to keep a high level of enthusiasm. In addition, goals make it easy for you to say no. The word "no" should be an important part of your vocabulary if you intend to achieve your goals. Many times, it is what you do *not* do that makes you successful.

For example, when ZAP Futures was started, we had a clearly articulated goal: Introduce a high-speed electronic order entry system that was accurate, easy to use, and compatible with other software. With our understanding of available technology, we shaped our goal around what we believed the people wanted rather than what we could supply them. Additionally, our goal for ZAP Futures was to shape itself around our *perception* of what the customer of the future would want. In many industries, companies merely hope to capture new market share by improving their existing product lines. In our case, we wanted to redefine the manner in which an industry conducts itself by supplying products to an industry that was just beginning to take form.

Our job was facilitated because we had well-defined goals that allowed us to include and exclude potential ideas and plans. As an analogy, consider the following: Before you take an automobile trip from Chicago to LA, you should get a road map and plan your trip. There would be certain points of interest that you would like to see along the way; some will be close to the main road and some will be far off it. It is up to you to decide how far out of your way you will go to see a certain point of interest. If the point of interest is very far off the main road, you must determine whether the detour is worth the delay in reaching your final destination. In the process of developing ZAP, many different people tried to divert us to their particular "point of interest." Most of the diversions, although interesting, were not within our strategy to reach our goal, and it was easy for us to say no! We were able to focus on the ideas that made sense and would help us reach our final destination.

Did we miss opportunities when we chose to take a pass on the diversions people offered us? Probably, but we never got sidetracked, we never got lost, and, most importantly, we never lost sight of our goal. Getting sidetracked by diversions is only one way people lose sight of their goals.

Probably the most problematic issue with goal setting is ending up with ill-defined goals. An old adage says that a problem well defined is half-solved. A corollary to that adage could be a goal well defined is half-achieved. Sometimes we set goals without thinking them through, and the goals are fuzzy, overly broad, or simply unrealistic. Part of the goal-setting strategy is to understand who you are, what your abilities are, how you approach problems, and what the real goal is. The simpler and more articulated the goal is, the easier it is to achieve. If you approach goal setting with a clearly defined purpose, you are much more likely to succeed and to have an easier time achieving success. Remember, goal setting is not a test of wills or an attempt to achieve the impossible.

Traders who set realistic goals have a benchmark against which they can judge their progress. However, even that is not enough. Setting the goal and seeing the end is not the same as reaching the goal. Setting a goal with a vision is only half the process. It is still very easy to lose your way and become confounded and frustrated. Think of a bee in a jar. If you place a bee in an open jar lying on its side with the bottom of the jar facing the sun, the bee will try to go through the bottom of the jar to get to the sun. The bee does not realize that if it turned around and crawled out of the opening that it would have an easier time flying toward the sun. Doing those things that are necessary to execute the goal is the second half of success.

There are many acronyms used to describe the process of goal setting and execution. Ours is **WATER.** "W" is for "write." You have to write down you goals. If you do not write them down, they are not fixed; they are not part of who you are as a person or a trader. Trading rooms are full of 3 × 5 cards taped to computers as constant reminders. The process of writing down your goals will help you narrow and shape them. "A" is for "act." Writing down your goals without a plan of action to bring them to fruition is only an exercise. Follow-through is part of the plan. Writing out the action necessary to achieve the goal is essential. A written plan of action is the road map. Your actions should be as clear as your goals and as simply expressed as your goals. "T" is for "tracking." Tracking your progress toward your goals is an evaluation process. Tracking is like taking your pulse. You find out how you are, how far along you are toward your goals, and what milestones or benchmarks you have reached. "E" is for "evaluating." Evaluating is the by-product of tracking and allows you to make an objective determination on the whole process, not just on how far along you are. You may find that you are on track. You may also find that you are way off track. In either event, you move on to "R." "R" is for "restate and refine." In the same way that writing is mostly rewriting, goal setting and executing strategies are mostly restating and refining what you have learned. Take advantage of the final steps to draw your focus even sharper on the end goal.

As a trader, make sure your goal setting and your executing strategies are realistic. As we said, goal setting is not a test to see if you can achieve the impossible. That is what your third-grade teacher had in mind when she told you to sit still and be quiet. Goals without time frames are useless. Time frames are more important than dollar figures. To set as a goal that you are going to make $100,000 day-trading bonds is a realistic goal. To set as a goal that you are going to make $100,000 day-trading bonds in 1 month is probably not a realistic goal. You know your abilities, your temperament, your level of skill, and your market knowledge. Create goals for the person you see in the mirror every morning, not the idealized version of the person you imagine in your daydreams.

Discipline

The most important step in reaching goals is doing something about them. Doing requires discipline. Remember the old adage: "The road to Hell is paved with good intentions"? The same holds true for the road to goals. The primary strategy for reaching goals is to have the discipline to achieve them. Discipline requires understanding and preparation. You must understand who you are, what your trading temperament is, and how to do the homework necessary to choose the system or methodology that is going to be best suited to your personality. Regardless of the system or methodology you use, it should in the first instance be automated with objective signals so that you can react with confidence. This applies to black boxes as well as to indicators. If you are simply going to shoot from the hip, you can stop reading now.

Automation will make decision making easier because it will allow you to respond to signals with confidence and an eye on your goals. When a trading signal comes, you must take that signal without any hesitation. More likely than not, you will lose more money by indecision than by the wrong decision. Discipline requires patience. You have to wait for opportunities based on your system, strategy, and trading plan. Your plan should be internally consistent and organized to allow you to limit losses while giving you a reasonable profit potential. If you are well prepared and have done you homework, you will have confidence in your system and your ability to execute it.

You should always be positive, relaxed, focused, and confident when you are trading. If you are negative, anxious,
nervous, and unfocused, you will find yourself swaying from
your goal and you *will* trade by whim and end up confused
about what to do next. If this occurs, stop trading. Review
your plan and your goals and refocus yourself to get back on
the road to success. It is important to remember that success
does not happen overnight. Recently, at a seminar, we told the
audience that it is very hard to make your first million; it takes
a lot of discipline. When asked how many people were working on making their first million, all the members of the audience raised their hands except one lady sitting in the front row.
We asked her if she already made her first million, and she
replied, "No, but when you told me how hard the first million
would be to make I figured I'd just start on my second million." Everyone got a good laugh, but the assumption under-
scores the discipline of one step at a time. By having a good
self-image, well-defined goals, and discipline, your chances
for success are multiplied exponentially.

CHAPTER 5

The Psychological Indicators

There are entire books and chapters in other books dedicated to the "psychology of trading." Most of them reiterate the basics: Plan your trade; trade your plan; don't become emotionally involved with the trade; etc. We review some of these points when discussing psychological tendencies because you cannot accurately describe the psychology of trading in a vacuum. You have to consider the personality and, more importantly, the behavior of the trader. Regarding the new "in-group" of modern electronic traders, are they different from the traders of yesterday who called in their orders? Are they different because they are armed with vast amounts of instant information, analysis, and computing power? Are their chances for success increased? The answer is yes and no.

Traders in the past were both successful and unsuccessful, just as traders using electronics are today. To some extent, the differences between past and present traders, and between success and failure lie not only in the system and the trader's ability, but also in the trader's personality, discipline, and response to the outside world. Discipline is an essential factor in following a regimented plan for success. Perhaps the speed, access, and power created by electronics have formed the "new" trader's personality and likewise have created a different breed of trader. Oddly enough, however, one's own psychology (our profile) is usually the last factor to be considered in trading.

We assume that we are who we are and let it go at that. Regardless of what our own determination of fair value for a market might be, we are still subject to outside influences as reflected in that market, and those outside influences inform our decisions about trading. Like Beanie Babies, some Internet stocks may have certain faddish qualities and their value, despite what we think, may be questionable, but the market is always right despite the character and effect of our own psychological indicators.

Let's examine these psychological indicators. That psychological indicators are as valid as technical indicators and fundamental factors in the total trading equation should not be an issue. If a trader is a gambler at heart, is subject to impulsive behavior, is influenced by group or mass behavior, reacts to peer pressure, follows fads, tries to time speculative bubbles, or gets caught up in media-induced opinions or trades while experiencing euphoria, depression, and/or illusions, these psychological indicators will be ever present.

Before discussing the different categories of psychological indicators, let's examine the one pot into which virtually all futures traders are thrown: trading as gambling. Despite the popular perception, there is a big difference between trading and gambling. Many people argue that playing the markets is equivalent to gambling. We disagree. Some people, however, say they are traders when actually they are gamblers. They are taking a shot at the markets because they have a hunch, have picked up a tip somewhere, or have fallen for the options salesperson's pitch on heating oil and unleaded gas. On the other hand, there are many people who claim to "play the market" who are not gamblers. Terminology does not define them. The difference between these two groups may lie in their approach, and the results are predictable.

In casino gambling, every game, from the slot machines to the roulette wheel, has what is known as a "negative outcome." That means if you put 1000 quarters into a slot machine that has a 95 percent payout, you would end up with approximately 950 quarters. Think about that. When people play slot machines, they are always looking for the machine that pays out the highest percentage. Actually they are looking for the machine where they will lose the least. When you bet on sports at the casinos (or through your "guy"), there is always a point spread. That is what the house makes. Everything you do at a casino produces a negative outcome. Granted, in certain games, like blackjack, you can count cards and move the odds in your favor. With that as the exception, the only reason you should be in a casino is to have fun. In the end, you can include yourself in the statistical average of casino goers who lose money.

When traders look at the markets, however, their normal expectation is for a "positive outcome." This expectation is not a guarantee. However, the average return on longer-term investing is a respectable 10 percent even when commissions are factored in. During the past few years, the results have been much better than that with the markets, rising to about 20 percent per year. We could easily expect to see those same results for the next 5 to 10 years. But by reducing trading to gambling, you are taking an anticipated positive outcome and turning it into an almost certain negative outcome.

One of the characteristics of an impulsive or a gambling personality is the inability to maintain positions for the long term. Unless you are day-trading with a plan, the shorter your time frame for a trade, the more like gambling it becomes. The idea of making a small sum of money on many trades as opposed to a large sum of money on very few trades can turn a positive income potential into a negative income reality.

This reminds us of the story about two bums talking on a park bench. The first bum says, "My wife left me and took everything I owned. Why are you here?" The second bum replies, "I was a day trader. I used to buy commodities at the low of the day and then sell them later on the same day at the highs." The first bum, looking puzzled, asks, "If you were such an astute trader, why are you sitting here with me? Why don't you live in a penthouse somewhere?" The second bum responds, "Commissions." A general rule is the length of the term you trade is directly proportionate to your failure rate. For short-term trades, with commissions and potential slippage on each trade, you would need significantly more winners than losers to avoid a negative income in the long run.

Understanding why investing can become gambling, let's take a closer look at the psychological indicators and how they might affect your trading.

Gambling and Impulsive Behavior

Many traders rationalize short-term trades by saying that they have good potential. That rationalization may be just a disguise to conceal the gambling aspects of their thought process. The truth of the matter is that most traders who are really gamblers do not have a clear idea of what price values should be because they lack objective evidence. Most information the average person receives is either from news stories or from biased vendors seeking a profit and does not provide a solid basis upon which to base price and value. Assuming that short-term traders are doomed to a negative outlook, why do they do it? For these "investors," the thought of not trading (read "gambling") is a crushing psychological disappointment. The results are secondary; the action is primary.

This type of compulsive behavior is obviously not new and is endemic to many endeavors. The trader as gambler is only one of such behavior's many guises. It has been estimated that three out of four people will place a bet of some type this year. In the view of the world, whether one gambles at a casino or just buys a lotto ticket is irrelevant. The world not only accepts gambling; it is enticed by it. Gambling for gambling's sake may be fine as long as one realizes that certain types of shorter-term trading are also gambling.

Within the gambling category there is a more severe area, and that is compulsive gambling. Like most compulsions, gambling can become an obsession and lead to a state of total ruin. So what starts out as a simple bet escalates to a point where the gambler risks not only money but also his or her family. Estimates are that 3 to 5 percent of the U.S. population are compulsive gamblers, which would mean that we have as many as 20 million compulsive gamblers here in the United States alone. It is likely that a large portion of those 20 million compulsive gamblers are also investing (gambling) in the markets. If they are playing the markets, then they will probably have to justify their decision by finding some research or news item that rationalizes the investment. The need for sound reasons to invest is not that important. The research or news story is enough to help rationalize the faulty decision. At the point when the trade goes bad, emotions and stress will enter the picture. During a period of stress the gambling preoccupation progresses and increases significantly. When you hear about a trader "blowing up" or losing a lot of money with a large-size position, it is easy to see the large-size position; it is easy to see the psychological reasoning (or lack of) that went through that person's mind while in the process of self-destruction.

Fad or Speculative Bubble

An example of a fad or speculative bubble is illustrated by what is occurring with certain toys that have become popular over the past few years. Beanie Babies is one fad that we all can relate to. To a large extent, the fad bubble occurred because of a supply-demand situation that was created by the manufacturer of this doll. By keeping production low, a secondary collectible market was established immediately by children, and even more so by children's parents who paid more and more as a result of increased prices. The Beanie Babies themselves became irrelevant; only the price increases had any significance. As people observed the price increases, they became envious of other people making money who had bought Beanie Babies earlier. Price increases fed on themselves and caused additional price increases as the promise of cash continued. Every day in the newspapers there were hundreds of advertisements offering to buy and sell Beanie Babies at ridiculous prices. Beanie Babies went from their original $5 retail price to hundreds and thousands of dollars in a 2- to 3-year period.

After the price of Beanie Babies hit its high, the prices started dropping precipitously due to the lack of further price increases. So it was the observation of price increases and the instant cash that it created that fed the price increases. When the highs were hit, prices fell because buying the already high-priced collectibles would not create wealth.

Beanie Babies are used in this example for one simple reason. You can live without a Beanie Baby. But you can't live without food and oil. In the early and mid-nineties, corn and crude oil had large price increases The increase in corn was because of a heat wave, and the increase in crude oil was a result of the Gulf War. One might argue that both these commodities are essentials for life. Although we agree with that assumption, how much of the price rise in corn from $2 to over $5 resulted from the fear of not eating and how much was the speculative fever that swept the grain markets during the heat wave? The rise would be about equal. Half the price increase was attributed to the fundamentals of smaller supply, but the other half was driven by a profit motive. So in addition to the fundamentals and technicals, there are also price movements based almost purely on the psychological perceptions of where the market will go.

Group or Mass Behavior

Group or mass behavior can influence the decisions we make in both positive and negative ways. In the positive sense, groups that are similar have similar trading habits. Systems are set up to help traders gather information to make intelligent trading decisions. Some system designers and developers have support or help groups that meet formally or use chat rooms on the Web. These support groups allow traders to discuss both positive and negative situations they have experienced using a particular trading system. This type of group situation is very controlled, and all the information is originating from or at least being monitored by the individual or company that developed the system. In this case you would expect the advice or information being presented to be accurate due to the controlled environment. These support or help groups will allow more accurate information to be filtered to the groups so that more intelligent trading decisions can be made. Also people feel secure in larger numbers, and you might act more deliberately if you knew that other traders were reacting the same way with similar results. This feeling of confidence is further substantiated when the group and system you are working with are profitable. People in groups will take more and greater risks than they would as individuals. In this controlled environment this increased risk effect can be positive because the group is being directed to trade a systematic approach.

Groups can also act in a very detrimental way by making disastrous judgments and decisions simply because group dynamics often create peer pressure, which in turn causes faulty reasoning. Studies have shown that a group will concentrate on facts and information that will support the dominant attitude of the group.

This behavior is illustrated in a study of 10 people in one room. They were all given three cards with numbers and colors on them. The card labeled #1 was red, #2 was yellow, and #3 was green. Nine of the people in the group were told to answer brown no matter what color they really saw, and the tenth person was given no special instruction and was also not told that the other nine people would always answer brown regardless of the color they saw. They were all placed at a large round table, and the participants were told to place card #1, which was red, face up in front of them. The first nine participants all turned a red #1 card, but stated it was brown as they had been instructed to. The tenth participant also said brown in over 75% of the tests.

Pressure to conform to the group was so overwhelming that the tenth participant was forced to agree with the group even though he or she knew with all certainty that the decision was wrong. The fear of rejection, of not being accepted, of being called crazy, and of going against the norm are some of the psychological factors at work. Most of the tenth participants went on to call the yellow #2 card and the green #3 brown card in spite of the fact that they knew they were wrong.

This same principle was operating when, just before Pearl Harbor was bombed, high-ranking Pentagon officials met with the President to discuss the possibility that Japan would attack the United States and force us out of our neutral stance and into World War II. The President was assured that the United States had such an overwhelming military superiority that there was no chance that Japan would ever consider such an option. No one would consider being deemed unpatriotic by opining that the U.S. military was not a superior force. Those who did would be quickly suppressed by self-appointed censors. Everyone agreed that Japan would not attack and patted each other on the back. The military was not placed on high alert. The next morning, Sunday, Pearl Harbor was bombed. The ill-fated meeting and its results are now known in psychological parlance as the "Pearl Harbor complex." It is a classic study in group behavior.

Media-Induced Opinions

Now more than ever, the media have an overwhelming influence on virtually all aspects of our lives. Commercials we see are strong influences on our spending habits. The food we eat, the clothes we wear, the places we go, the cars we drive, and so on are determined, for the most part, by what is perceived to be the norm. Most people do not have an independent basis for objective judgment. We turn to people we perceive to be in charge as reported by the media for our information. In many cases we are reduced to mere spectators, voyeurs.

The media can influence us and can change us. As the media continue to report a story, they solidify it and make it that much more important. When there is a disaster, financial or otherwise, we turn to the media for a sense of common experience. "Good" politicians and successful companies have learned to manipulate the media to their advantage. We turn to the media to see the "experts" and validate the decisions we are making. There are enough experts out there so you will definitely find one that agrees with your thinking.

The media also benefit from the distribution of wealth and power, and thus it is in their best interest to report on as many areas of the same story that they believe the public will accept. The media create news from news. In the print media, if you don't have something to say, you can make your paper two or three pages shorter. When you are reporting news on TV, you cannot have dead air time so the practice of creating news from news is even more important. The power of the media, especially TV can never be underestimated.

When you ask people where they heard a certain piece of news and they answer TV, we tend to accept it without further qualification. Publication to the world adds instant credibility to almost anything. We react, and external actions follow. How many times have you read a paper or heard something on TV and then reacted based on that story? The last place to look for trading signals would be in the media, unless the only thing you are doing is rationalizing your investment decision. The majority is not always right. If it was, we would all be rich.

6

How to Choose the Right System

There are two competing factors in any decision-making process: your intellect and your emotion. Intellect is not intended to be understood as meaning "intellectual," but rather as objective reasoning and subject to rational reflection. In the same sense, emotion is not to be understood as "irrational," but rather as reactive to ongoing events. The tug between the two, for most people, is a natural process. In trading, this "natural process" becomes exaggerated because of risk. If trading were merely a matter of deciding whether to buy or sell with no consequences, this natural process would be a no-brainer. You would get in the market (long or short), wait to see what happens, reverse when you are wrong, and go home a bit wiser but no poorer, or no richer. Money muddies up the whole process.

Without the money, being right or wrong is riskless. There are no consequences. With money thrown into the equation, there are definite consequences, and they are real. Moreover, without the proper "mindset" for actual trading, you subject yourself to the insidious "law of unintended consequences." The proper mindset for trading ensures that intellect is the dominant factor for many. This mindset, however, is not always easy to achieve even under normal circumstances. When the whole trading mix is fueled with emotion (pure adrenaline), intellect takes a backseat.

All is not lost, however. If you understand the importance of having both a plan and a goal before you trade, and if you are cognizant of the patterns of behavior that characterize and influence your actions, you can become a competent trader. By fully comprehending your psychological predisposition, you can plan to avoid known pitfalls and thereby more astutely formulate a plan for success. We all know that trading involves self-imposed discipline. It does not come from outside; it comes from within. However, anyone who has traded also knows that trading is a surefire way to expose every emotional loose end and frayed tether in your genetic makeup. The adrenaline rush of the unknown that you experience when trading is similar to that experienced by both regulars and novices in Las Vegas. You see and hear about winning and losing money, and you think "that could be me." The crowd at the craps table generates enthusiasm, and you want to participate with the group.

These folks, including you, are acting 100 percent from emotions, and if that is the way you trade the futures markets, don't ever give up your day job. Nevertheless, knowing in advance that you have certain emotional tendencies (which, by the way, we all do), you can plan to avoid them. Understanding these tendencies can help you to avoid the psychological pitfalls that are the downfall of many traders. Mental conditioning will help give you confidence, anxiety control, and personal motivation and allow you to focus on following your system for, or approach to, the markets without the weight of emotional clutter spilling into your decision making.

How, then, do you determine whether you are dominated by your intellect or your emotion? Let's do an exercise to find out. Following is a list of 30 pairs of words. Circle the word in each pair that best describes you. Be honest, and select the one that characterizes you. If you believe that they both describe you, select the one that is most like you. If you believe neither one describes you, then select the one that is the least objectionable. Take the test quickly. Do not think about the words too much. Go with your first reaction. ***There are no right or wrong answers.*** The point of this exercise is not to rate you as good or bad; it simply helps you define your natural tendencies. With this understanding you can then come to trading with a system or approach that at least complements, rather than confounds, your personality.

daring	trusting
persistent	accurate
stubborn	obliging
cultured	vigorous
outspoken	restrained
cheerful	charming
talkative	conventional
accurate	competitive
patient	sociable
assertive	moderate
sympathetic	convincing

inspiring	adaptable
confident	agreeable
determined	cautious
optimistic	peaceful
eager	contented
fearful	unconquerable
decisive	controlled
gentle	playful
obedient	pioneering
good-natured	lighthearted
aggressive	accommodating
companionable	generous
loyal	self-reliant
attractive	submissive
kind	bold
high-spirited	positive
nervy	even-tempered
tolerant	good mixer
open-minded	receptive

Self-Scoring

daring	E	trusting	I
persistent	E	accurate	I
stubborn	E	obliging	I
cultured	I	vigorous	E
outspoken	E	restrained	I
cheerful	I	charming	E
talkative	E	conventional	I
accurate	I	competitive	E

patient   I

assertive   E

sympathetic   I

inspiring   E

confident   E

determined   E

optimistic   E

eager   E

fearful   I

decisive   E

gentle   I

obedient   I

good-natured   I

aggressive   E

companionable   E

loyal   I

attractive   E

kind   I

high-spirited   I

nervy   E

tolerant   I

open-minded   E

sociable   E

moderate   I

convincing   E

adaptable   I

agreeable   I

cautious   I

peaceful   I

contented   I

unconquerable   E

controlled   I

playful   E

pioneering   E

lighthearted   E

accommodating   I

generous   I

self-reliant   E

submissive   I

bold   E

positive   E

even-tempered   I

good mixer   E

receptive   I

How to score: Count up the number of times you chose the I (intellect) word and the number of times you chose the E (emotion) word. Compare the two. If you have 16 or more I or E words, that tendency indicates your personality predisposition.

Now that you have completed the exercise, let's examine your natural psychological tendencies. These tendencies fall into one of three categories:

High I. This category is characterized by *intellect* as the controlling factor.

High E. This category is characterized by *emotion* as the controlling factor.

Equal E and I. This category is characterized by both emotion and intellect in almost equal proportions and probably exists only in a parallel universe somewhere or in the minds of those who don't like the results of the exercise. But more about them later.

Let's look at what your specific tendencies hold in store for you and how you can use that information to build a plan of action to make you a more competent trader.

High-E Tendencies

Assuming for the moment that your score on the exercise places you in the category for high-E tendencies, what does this tell you? High-E tendencies fall in the "want to" category. High-E people want to generate enthusiasm, want to make a favorable impression, want to help others, want to take authority, want to solve problems, want to work in a group, want to make quick decisions, and want to get immediate results. The issue is whether their wants are satisfied. Wanting to and doing are not always mirror images of the same desire. Why is that? High-E individuals tend to be emotional, anxious, and generally subject to confusion about what exactly they should do. One thing is for sure, however; they do not want anyone telling them what to do.

Consequently, high-E individuals are hesitant; they talk about planning, they act on whims, and in trading, they cannot seem to rely on a constant methodology. And the failure to focus on and to follow a constant methodology is probably the single most corrosive high-E tendency associated with failure. High-E individuals are second-guessers by nature and would rather rely on intuition (what feels right at that moment) than on what the long-term or the short-term indicators might tell them.

Some high-E traders may exhibit a type A personality profile because they want to advance themselves along the learning curve via shortcuts, be recognized by their peers, compete in the marketplace (against the market in most instances), and turn out to be like the overachiever next door. The problem for these traders is they also usually have poorly defined goals, go with their gut feel, are hurried and anxious to finish a project, and are easily upset when they are wrong. The good news, however, is that with the right preparation and clear thinking (counterintuitive though it may be), high-E traders can also become successful traders.

High-E Approach for Success

If you are a high-E trader and realize you are holding the emotional hand, you need to adjust your emotional compass before you quit your day job to trade full time. To develop your competence as a trader, you will have to undertake those "life changes" that will support your efforts to pace yourself and allow you to approach the trading day with a more relaxed perspective. Approach all days with equal anticipation and with equal resolve. For instance, just because a "number" is due out on a particular day does not make that day any more special than any other trading day. Events affecting the market occur every day. Your mental preparation should be always on game, decisive, and ready to trade. As a high-E trader you should find a system that will give you some objectivity in the decision-making process. The system or methodology you select should be one that provides you with a set of indicators from which and around which you can build your trading day. You will be more satisfied with this type of system rather than one that provides you with specific trades. If you choose a system or approach to the markets that gives you specific trades (even though the system might be a good one), you will probably second-guess it.

Even with high-E tendencies and an indicator system or methodology, it is important to develop the ability to respond (not react) quickly, with confidence, and with a positive approach when you get a trading signal. Be conscious of the rules that the indicator system or methodology sets out and apply them in a consistent manner. Developing an indicator system and learning to navigate its rules is pointless if you are going to constantly override the indicators. Notwithstanding the fact that such systems are not black boxes and do give you the benefit of adjusting the trade according to the indicators, it is still critical that you respect the rules for that particular system. If you are not going to be consistent in your approach, give your money to someone else to trade for you.

Identify and interact with a group of people following the same system or methodology. Not only will this quicken your understanding of the potential problem areas into which high-E individuals wander, but it will also give you the positive experience of participating in a group. This is not to imply, however, that all who may be following a particular system are high-E individuals. Through your interaction with other traders in a group you will acquire a sense of how they respond to signals and the respect that they afford the rules for the system. Again, identification with a user or discussion group (chat room) where a system or methodology is the common denominator does not guarantee your success with the system. Such identification, however, will afford you a broad base of knowledgeable users from and with whom you can learn.

High-E individuals also seem to thrive on difficult assignments that require priorities and deadlines. High-E individuals are good (some might say obsessive) record keepers and are very conscious of order (even though they might question it). A system that imposes on you the need to maintain an orderly approach to the markets will help you to focus on responding to market situations rather than reacting to them. Such a plan will also prevent you from trying to trade the markets you wish you had, rather than the ones you have. We cannot tell you how many times we have had discussions with traders who tell us what they would have done "if only the markets would have done" this or done that.

By adopting these approaches to action, you will be making it easier for you to follow your system or methodology. Systems will mathematically define, quantify, and categorize past relationships in collective human behavior and give you a statistical probability for the future. Remember, indicator systems or methodologies will not take the emotion out of you. You are who you are. But these indicator systems will help take the operational emotional stress out of your trading, and that in and of itself will increase your chances of competence.

High-I Tendencies

If you find yourself in the high-I category, you also have issues to consider and probable adjustments to make in your trading approach. High-I individuals are not that different from high-E individuals. It's just that your psychological wiring runs on a different level, and as a result, you have a different perspective on almost everything, including the markets. Assuming the quantitative nature of the markets as revealed in the vast majority of all systems or methodologies, it is not understanding the markets that differentiates the high I's from the high E's. Instead, high E's and high I's come to the markets with different psychological profiles.

High-I individuals tend to be critical thinkers. Critical in this sense is not to be viewed as prone to criticism, but as analytical in the scientific sense. High I's believe that there is a scientific order in the repetitive nature of the markets. High I's understand that the markets duplicate themselves and, under the same circumstances, will, more likely than not, produce the same or similar results. Thus, as critical thinkers, high I's will allow a system or methodology to find the recurring pattern in the market and, by overlaying a known or preprogrammed matrix, produce the desired results. In this sense, high I's, unlike high E's, are not second-guessers. They do what the system tells them to do.

High-I individuals also concentrate on details and are very patient. Every piece of market data is important, and none is to be left out. Elimination of details (data) is to be determined only by the system or methodology, not by the individual. High I's understand that it is not immediately important what they think about either the system or the approach they are using. The only important issue is whether the variables that make up the system or methodology are properly set to capture the projected move for a particular bar, or hour, or day, or trend.

For instance, it is not important for high I's whether a 5-day moving average or a 10-day moving average is a programmed variable in the system. As a high I, you will use either one as long as there is an underlying quantitative justification for its use and the system dictates that justification based on a historical pattern or calculation. One algorithm is as meaningful as the next. A high E, on the other hand, will wrestle with the decision about which historical time period should work best and why it should work best. A high I simply does not care. There will be no wringing of hands or gnashing of teeth for the high I. If the system or methodology calls for a 5-day moving average under the set of circumstances labeled "X," then a 5-day moving average it is, regardless of what you may think about its use under that set of circumstances.

High-I individuals are also characterized by specialized skills. This is not to be thought of as the "skill sets" that human resource people like to check off on job applications and that fill the pages of the social sciences. Rather, the skill sets and specialized knowledge at issue here are more deeply rooted in the individual personality than those skills you "learn." This specialized knowledge could include a facility with numbers, language, music, or the visual arts. There is a certain intuitiveness in the source of these skills. You know it if you have them; and if you are a high E, you bemoan the fact that you do not possess them. High E's somehow sense that the "special knowledge" skills are gifts of which they have been deprived.

This is not an easy category to articulate in terms of high-I traders. There may appear to be internal inconsistencies. For example, if you argue that an individual is an accomplished artist and therefore possesses a specialized skill, does that necessarily lead to the conclusion that such a skill will help that individual be a better trader? Or to put it more bluntly, is someone who is good with numbers going to be a better trader than someone who is good with languages but can't balance a checkbook? Who will be a more competent trader is probably the wrong question. Understanding your tendencies is what will help you become a more competent trader, not setting up left-brain versus right-brain dichotomies to disprove that artists can trade as well as engineers.

However, for you purists, there is a reactive phenomenon that may help to distinguish between the specialized skills of the humanist and those of the scientist. This has to do with the need for subjective control and participation. As we have seen in suggesting the type of system or methodology for high E's, one that allows them to participate in the decision making, just the opposite can be posited for you high I's. As we will see in the following section, following exact directions and focusing on an automatic pattern of decision making that is predetermined will make it easier for high I's to stay focused and trade without distraction.

High-I Approach for Success

As part of the high-I approach for success in trading, it is probably wise to limit your search for systems or methodologies to those that will generate specific trading signals. More likely than not, these systems or approaches will be black boxes. The black-box systems are plug and play. With these systems and methodologies the trader simply follows directions and places the trades when the system generates a signal. The farther away you get from these black boxes, the closer you get to high-E systems. Since computerized trading systems have been available to the retail public on a mass scale, the range of systems has been described in a scale from black boxes to gray boxes to white boxes. As you move toward the white-box end of the scale, you get closer to systems that are indicators only and do not give specific signals.

It is also prudent to use several trading systems that generate specific trading signals rather than just one system. Multiple systems offer you the opportunity to compare the basis for the signals generated. Obviously, you should structure these systems so that you are comparing apples to apples and not apples to oranges. Day-trading systems are going to give you a much different picture of the market than long-term trend-following systems. High I's will enjoy the comparative nature of this approach, whereas high E's may not.

High-I traders are more apt to follow a mid-term or a long-term trading strategy because of their greater degree of patience. Certainly there are high E's who also follow mid-term and long-term strategies. But in general, high I's are more likely to be satisfied with this type of approach. By following one mid-term and one longer-term system, the comparative analysis will be more appealing to high I's. Regardless of your choice, limit the number of systems you follow and execute the trading signals precisely. Look for a system that is traditional nuts and bolts and not too fancy. Bells and whistles are nice, and may have some utilitarian value. However, relatively straightforward, totally automatic systems that generate specific trading points and have standard operating procedures are, in the long run, going to suit you better.

The Internet has made communication among traders immediate and continuous. Discussion groups for systems followers abound and are often sponsored by system vendors. While not a sine qua non for high-I traders, participation in discussion groups does offer a perspective and sense of community from which all traders can profit. Although the discussions in these groups run from the sublime to the arcane, if you are a gray-box high-I trader whose system requires some subjective interpretation, you will encounter traders who share your view and thus provide support. Even if you view yourself as "the lone trader" who does not want any outside interference, you will find willing correspondents in these groups with whom you can discuss you ideas. It is this like-mindedness in another trader that will lend a level of support in the development of your competence.

One final note regarding the potential success for high E's and high I's. Remember, the reason for determining whether you are a high I or a high E is not to point you in the direction of the trading's holy grail. There isn't one. The point of the exercise and suggestions is to help you determine who you are and how you might become a more competent trader. When you consider that there are literally hundreds if not thousands of commercially available trading systems, software programs, books, videos, and seminars from which to choose, selecting or devising the type of system that best suits your profile is as important as the system itself. Systems come and go, and a thousand factors affect the markets, but you are who you are, and that is not likely to change. Still, you can adapt with a conscious effort on your part.

Even Tendencies

If, after you have completed the personality profile exercise, you come up an "even," we suggest you redo the exercise. Although it is possible to be an even, it is unlikely. If you have followed the simple instructions (you I's out there) and have not tried to anticipate the answers in the exercise so you get it "right" (you E's out there), it is probable that you are either an E or an I. Even tendencies do not necessarily allow you to have the best of both worlds without the worst as well. As we stated, more than likely you are actually either an E or an I. It is important that you closely examine both your E and I tendencies and decide for yourself where you are most comfortable.

Being in the middle is probably not the most comfortable place. Although the middle may seem to offer the safest ground (terra firma that will let you pick and choose), it will probably turn out to be a no-man's-land when trying to devise a successful approach for trading. Why is that? Physiology provides the clue. When you factor the power of adrenaline into your decision-making character, it will increase your E tendencies.

Look closer at both your E tendencies and your I tendencies and determine which describe your personal profile the best. Employing the suggestions above, select or design a system that best fits your personality and trading goals. In the end, you need to be focused, relaxed, positive, and confident that your plan will work regardless of the system you choose. After all, the system or methodology you choose could be contrary to what you think is right. Even more frustrating would be agreeing with your system and discovering that both you and your system are wrong. The point is, do your homework before you buy or design a system and then do not second-guess it.

Act responsively and decisively on the trading signals in a consistent pattern. You, like most other serious traders, will see the big picture if you plan your trades, are well prepared, and are positive, confident, and focused. If the system you have selected is a lousy system, it does not mean you are in the wrong category. It simply means you have either purchased or designed a lousy trading system. Talk with other traders and systems developers. Let them help you find a reliable system. Ask for a free-trial period. Check out the historical performance of the system you choose. But that choice does not alone determine whether you will be a competent trader. The system you select may determine whether you make successful trades. If your system fails you, that is one thing. If you fail yourself in selecting the system that best suits your personality, that is another thing.

By designing a system that suits your personality, you are going to make the trading process easier and more fun and, it is hoped, more profitable. Understanding your tendencies will allow you to focus on your strengths and afford you a plan of action for your weaknesses. The anticipated result of this process is that by making the right choices based on who you are, you will tend to follow your system or methodology more accurately and thereby increase your chances for success. Once you fully understand your motives for trading, you will develop the positive state of mind, confidence, discipline, and patience necessary to follow that system or methodology in a consistent manner.

7

A Five-Step Plan for Successful Electronic Trading

E ven with a great trading system, it is paramount that you, the person pulling the trigger, be mentally prepared. You should have reviewed systems, narrowed down your choice, and selected a system that suits your personality. In addition to this, you should have your specific written goals and the action strategy necessary to achieve them. You should clear your mind of all negative thoughts and likewise don't look at the world through rose-colored glasses. It is now time to look at some of the technical components necessary to develop a successful online trading strategy. Before we examine the indicators and how they function, it is important to understand that no single indicator works successfully in isolation. It is the combination of indicators you use in designing your system that creates the whole picture of the market.

Certain indicators are *leading indicators*. Leading indicators help you to predict potential market action in advance.

Other indicators are *lagging indicators*. Lagging indicators will not give you an entry or exit signal until a trend has developed. As you will see, leading indicators react more immediately, so you are in and out of the market faster. However, with leading indicators you may miss the potential to capture a major trend. Lagging indicators are delayed and do not give signals until a trend, more likely than not, has reversed. As a result, you tend to give back a portion of the profit before you get out of an existing trade, and you enter a new trade later than you would like to. Needless to say, there are advantages and disadvantages to both leading and lagging indicators. However, combinations of leading and lagging indicators tend to filter each other when used properly. It is the alignment of all these indicators that will give you the highest probability of a winning trade.

In many cases it is not the trading signals you get that will make the system you've designed profitable. The signals that would have resulted in losing trades that the combination of indicators filtered out keep you from making sure losers. In the following chapters you will learn about some key technical indicators and how to properly apply them. It is important to learn the advantages and disadvantages of each and how each reacts to market changes. It is your understanding of these indicators and what they reveal about the market that will give you the confidence to trade successfully and with ongoing competence.

The following five-step plan provides an overview of the indicators discussed in the succeeding chapter. Review the plan both before and after you read Chapter 8 on indicators. Some of the references in the plan may seem out of context until you review Chapter 8.

The Five-Step Plan

1. Identify the trades that appear to have the best profit potential.
2. Analyze a potential trade in a systematic fashion.
3. Time each purchase to minimize risk and maximize reward.
4. Manage your portfolio to stay abreast of changes that might affect your trade.
5. Exit each position when the time is right.

1. Identify the trades that appear to have the best profit potential.

By tracking indicators that tend to work best in trending markets, you have a good probability to identify position trades. The duration of the trend and the timing of your entry into that trending market will obviously determine your profit. If you catch a developing trend, the profit potential is greater than if you catch only a portion of the trend. As you will see, sideways markets give few clues about a trend and require the one thing all traders wish they had, patience.

Moving averages are good indicators in determining the beginning stages of a trend and determining an established trend. As we will discuss later, the moving average crossover method can alert you to a developing trend and allow you to initiate a trade in the early stages of the trend. Moving averages can also identify a market that is already trending. Generally, when the short-, mid-, and longer-term moving averages are all moving in the same direction in a parallel fashion, the channel that develops indicates a trend is under way. Another indicator we will examine concerning trend development is the volume indicator. High volume in the direction of the trend and low volume in a support area or resistance area help in describing a trend and are factors to consider before placing a trade. If the trend is to hold, then volume should pick up as the market resumes its move in the direction of the trend. There will be more about this later.

2. Analyze a potential trade in a systematic fashion.

Analyze a potential trade in a systematic way by reviewing all your indicators. Look at the long-term indicators first so you can assess the bigger picture. In assessing the longer-term trend, you will generally have a better idea of the technical patterns and channels that are developing. There is less clutter on a longer-term chart than on the short-term chart. On the long-term charts, the areas of support and resistance will be more defined because the market will test those areas many times. After you have determined the long-term trend, create an overlay with the short-term indicators as a timing mechanism. Note where the bottoms or tops of the channels are. A buy signal generated from the shorter-term support and resistance areas with support from the indicators is a reasoned approach. By looking at the longer overall trend first and then using your shorter-term indicators as a timing mechanism, you will be able to time your trades for the most profit potential with the least amount of risk.

3. Time each purchase to minimize risk and maximize reward.

Time each purchase to minimize risk and maximize return. Timing is everything. Using both short- and long-term indicators as mentioned above, without due consideration to timing, could result in an unacceptable trading signal from a risk-reward perspective. The indicators will usually give you a trading signal based on the percentages for the success of that particular trade. However, these indicators neglect to calculate what a proper risk-reward ratio might be. If the probability is high that you will have a winning trade (above 70 percent), then you can use a lower risk-reward ratio such as *risk one–reward two*. If you are looking at winning percentages being under 70 percent, then you must look for less risk and higher profit potential of at least *risk one–reward three*. When you calculate your risk-reward formula, make sure you add commissions and slippage to your formula. Commissions are a fixed amount, but slippage depends on the market. Both can eat up a significant part of your potential profits.

4. Manage your portfolio to stay abreast of changes that might affect your trade.

Managing your portfolio means staying abreast of market changes that might affect your trade. When changes happen, you should be prepared to act in a preplanned and deliberate manner. News stories and government reports often have an immediate effect on the market. If the story or report is unexpected, it can create a dramatic change. Whether the change is lasting or temporary, the degree of change is a function of whether the market discounted the story (through rumor, for instance) or the report (via strategic "leaks") prior to release. Typically, immediately after a news story or government report is released, the market tends to have a knee-jerk reaction until there is a chance to absorb the full impact of the information. After this reaction, the market will generally continue with the trend it was in, although in some cases it may reverse to trade in a new direction. This is a time when you want to watch your indicators very closely for any early sign of a possible trend reversal.

5. Exit each position when the time is right.

Exit each position when the time is right, not too early and not too late. Remember, the decision to exit a losing trade is easier to make than with a profitable trade, particularly for you high I's. With a losing trade, you should be getting out with a predetermined loss, and there is nothing else to think about. You lost and you are out of the trade. Move on. With a winning trade, however, it is a different story. This is when the type-I tendencies take over. When you are making money, you are thinking about how high is high, or how low is low; or you may think that you can get out now and get in at a better price. As you will discover, there is an inexhaustible supply of rationales why you should get out of a winning trade. Do not do it. For example, if you have a trade with a $3000 profit and you get out because you believe the market will correct and then it doesn't, you will be trashing your risk-reward ratio. If the market continues in its trend and you have already gotten out, then any additional profit you did not take is in reality a loss. For example, if you could have made a total of $5000 and you only took $3000 out of the trade, then the extra $2000 is a loss against your overall trading plan.

If you get in the habit of getting out of trades early because of a hunch, you will find that the profits that you did not take can turn a profitable system into a losing one. It is very important to follow your system without deviation. Even though you believe that $3000 was a good profit, your system was designed to take a $5000 profit. If you give up a $2000 profit on five trades, then you have left $10,000 in profit on the table. This habit has just turned your good system into a loser and has turned you into a premature profit taker. Do not blame the system. Blame yourself.

8

The Core Indicators

You may decide to purchase a black-box system, to buy a gray-box software package that gives you indicators, or to create your own system. Regardless of the one you choose, an operational understanding of technical indicators—how they work and how to use them—is basic. Treatises and periodical articles on technical trading abound. Unless you are trading multiple complex strategies, which most of you are not, or need to be able to compute complicated equations, which most of you do not, a layperson's understanding of technical trading will suffice. If you want to become more proficient in the technical aspects of trading, many good seminars are available. Also, there are many proficient traders who participate in user and discussion groups who will gladly share their thoughts on the technical aspects of trading. In this chapter we will review the basic tenets of the most commonly used technical indicators.

Oscillators

The word "oscillator" comes from the Latin root *oscillum*, "to swing." The obvious denotation implies movement back and forth, and when applied to the markets, oscillators simply time volatility and direction. A variety of oscillators are available, occurring under different names. As a whole, they all function in a similar manner. If used properly, oscillators can alert you to potential short-term tops or bottoms in sideways or non-trending markets and can signal when a market is losing its momentum in a trending market. Oscillators, like most other indicators, should not be used alone. They are best used to verify other indicators. Oscillators are part of the array of analytical tools that a good trader employs to chart a strategy. Oscillators are also the most misused of all technical indicators because they are open for wide interpretation.

Most oscillators are constructed with upper and lower boundaries that have theoretical values ranging from –120 to 180 (see Figure 8-1) or –5 to +5 (see Figure 8-2), depending upon how the value of the indicator is calculated. As a general rule, when the oscillator approaches the upper end of the band, it suggests an overbought condition; and when it approaches the lower end of the band, it suggests an oversold condition. Thus, when the oscillator approaches the lower end of the band, you should be a buyer; and conversely, when the oscillator approaches the higher end, you should be a seller.

Most of the times these general rules hold true. *However, it is critical to understand that when there are strong trending markets, oscillators work in reverse.* A good example is the S&P 500 market, which has been in a strong uptrend for many years. If you compare price action to the oscillator, you will discover that some of the largest up moves occur when the

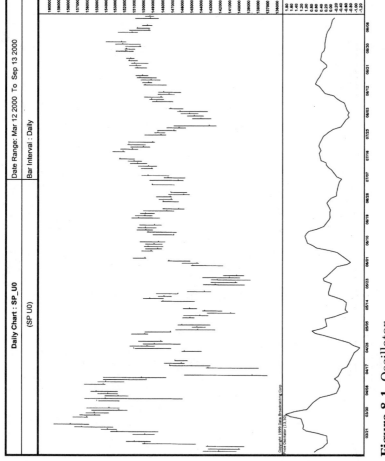

Figure 8-1 Oscillator

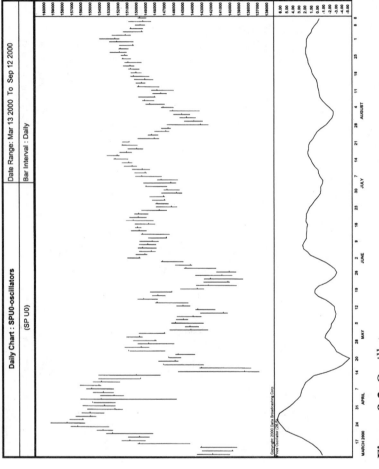

Figure 8-2 Oscillator

oscillator is at a high level. In strong trending markets oscillators actually tend to work well at extremes and should not be used the same way as in nontrending markets. *It is very important in a trending market that you only trade in the direction of the trend and ignore signals that are contrary to the trend.* The old saw "the trend is your friend" is as valid as it gets. The market is always right. You must exercise patience in trending markets. Once a trend is established, the longer it goes in that direction, the more it should be expected to continue in that same direction.

In a trending market, it is better to use oscillators as momentum indicators. Momentum indicators measure the rate of price change, as opposed to the actual price levels. As we look at the different types of oscillators, it is important to remember two critical points: Oscillator signals should only be taken if they are in the direction of the trend, and oscillators should be used in conjunction with other technical indicators. Now let's take a look at three popular oscillators: momentum indicators, stochastics, and the relative strength index.

Momentum Indicators

As a general rule, oscillators, except for momentum indicators, are lagging indicators. In other words, the price action of the market usually turns before the oscillator is able to give you an accurate signal. The speed and velocity at which a price reverses could cause you to stay in a position too long if you are relying only on oscillators that give you a late trading signal. Momentum indicators, however, always lead the price movement. Momentum indicators generally lead the rise or fall in price by at least 1 to 3 days (see Figure 8-3).

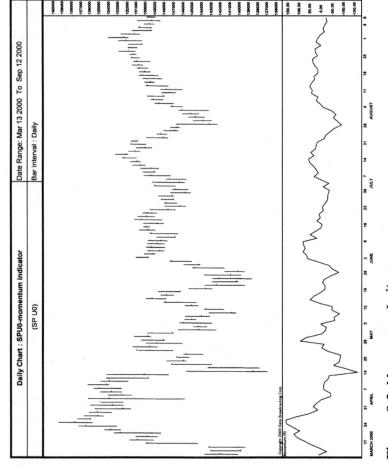

Figure 8-3 Momentum Indicators

The advantage of a momentum indicator is obvious: It tells you in advance when the velocity of a market is slowing and possibly reversing. By knowing when a market is going into a consolidation period or reversing its trend, you are able to get out of a trade and get in again at a better price or, perhaps, to reverse your position. The principal disadvantage of momentum indicators, as with all indicators, is the possibility of getting a false signal. In the case of a momentum indicator giving a false signal, and thereby causing you to get out too early or reverse a position that should not be reversed, you would have to reposition yourself at a new price or simply get out of the reversed position with a loss. Again, as with all oscillators, we want to emphasize that you should only take signals in the direction of the trend (see Figure 8-4).

The structure of the variables for determining momentum indicators is based on a historical time-frame interval. Most momentum oscillators use an interval time frame of between 10 and 20 days. (See Figures 8-5 and 8-6.) The greater the number of days in the variable, the smoother the momentum line will be. The downside to increasing the number of days that makes up the variable is that you create the possibility of lengthening the lag time. Obviously, if the lag time is too great, the signal will be generated after the fact.

The 10-day momentum indicator is the most commonly used time-frame variable. To calculate a 10-day momentum indicator you subtract the closing price 10 days ago from the latest closing price. This calculation will render either a positive or a negative number that is then plotted on a graph. If the most recent closing price is greater than the closing price 10 days ago (prices have gone higher), then you would have a positive number. If the last closing price is lower than the

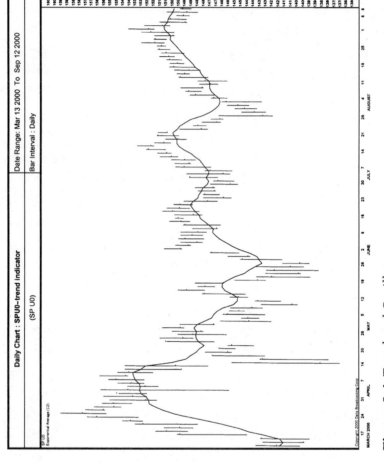

Figure 8-4 Trend and Oscillator

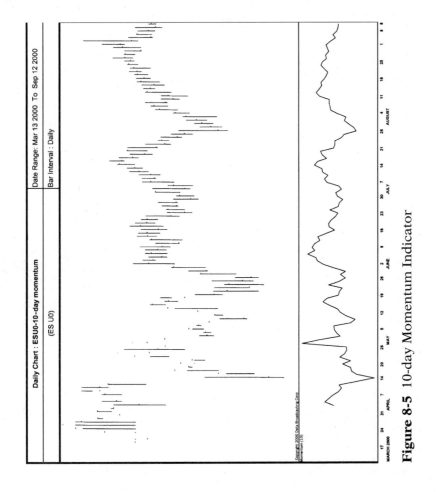

Figure 8-5 10-day Momentum Indicator

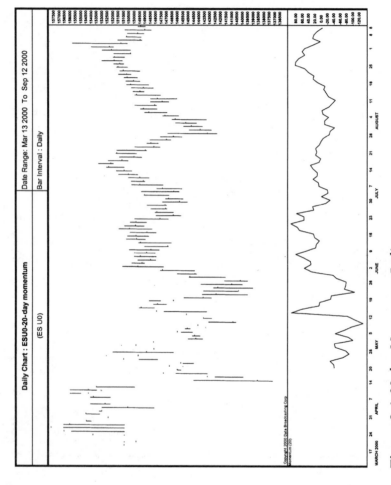

Figure 8-6 20-day Momentum Indicator

closing price 10 days ago (prices have gone lower), you would have a negative number. For example, if today's close was 52 and the close 10 days ago was 48, then a +4 value would be the result. However, if today's close was 48 and 10 days ago it was 52, then a –4 value would be plotted.

Momentum indicators also plot the rate (the velocity) at which prices are increasing or decreasing. When prices are increasing and the value of the momentum indicator is a positive number (see Figure 8-7), the market is accelerating to the upside. When the momentum line flattens out, the rate of ascent is leveling off. In other words, the most recent prices are the same as the gains achieved 10 days earlier. When the momentum begins to decrease but remains above the zero line, the uptrend is still viable even though it is losing momentum at a rapid rate. When the momentum line goes below the zero line (see Figure 8-8), the current close is below that of 10 days ago. When this occurs, it is an indication that a downward trend in prices has begun. As the momentum continues to decrease, you will usually see an acceleration of the downtrend. It is only when the line turns up again do you know that the downtrend is decelerating. Only when the momentum line goes above zero does the uptrend resume.

You can derive specific trading signals from a momentum oscillator in two different ways. However, we want to caution you that these specific trading signals should only be used when combined with other technical indicators. One method of generating buy or sell signals is to buy when the momentum line crosses above the zero line and sell when it crosses below the zero line. This crossover method will act as an overbought or oversold indicator and help you get out of your positions at the market extremes.

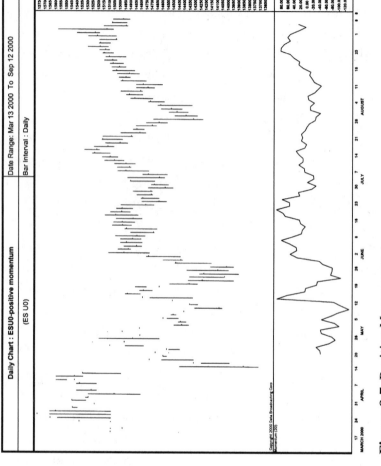

Figure 8-7 Positive Momentum

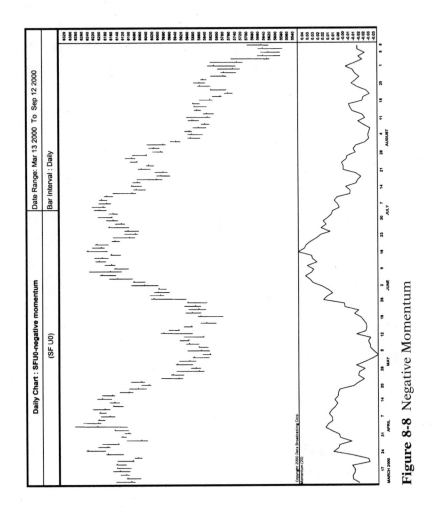

Figure 8-8 Negative Momentum

In order to formulate the upper and lower bands, look at the extreme highs and lows that the momentum oscillator band has historically produced. These extreme values would be given a value of +100 percent and 0 percent of both the upper and lower bands, respectively. Simply subtract 20 percent from the upper extreme to calculate the upper band, and add 20 percent to the lower extreme to calculate the lower band. When the prices rise above the upper band (+80 percent level), you would exit a long position (see Figure 8-9). Conversely, when prices fall below the lower band (20 percent level), you would exit short positions. Figure 8-10 illustrates this point.

You can exit a long position above the upper band (+80 percent), but do not go short. This is probably not a reversal situation, and if you think the market has topped and will go lower, chances are you will be wrong. Odds are if you are in a bull market when the price crosses above the upper band (+80 percent), the extreme prices will simply go into a congestion or sideways phase. In this scenario, you will be flat, waiting to receive another buy signal if the price crosses the 50 percent line to the upside. The momentum oscillator does an excellent job in defining gains or losses in momentum, but it is not as effective in defining upper and lower bands. We therefore recommend that, where possible, you use the other two oscillators described in this chapter—stochastics and relative strength index—to help detect extreme overbought and oversold conditions in the market.

Stochastics

Stochastics are an excellent way to time your trades with better accuracy. They prevent you from getting involved in an over-

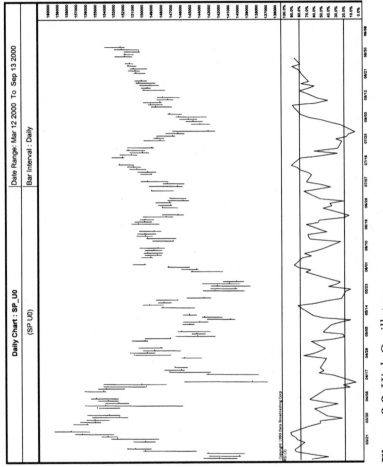

Figure 8-9 High Oscillator

89

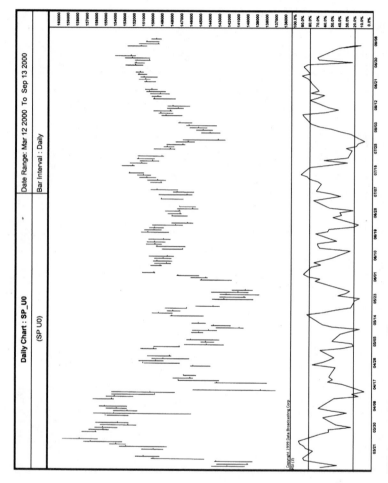

Figure 8-10 Low Oscillator

bought or oversold condition. Stochastics work extremely well during periods of consolidation. However, in strong trends these indicators can be misleading. Virtually all online charting services offer stochastics, and all you need to do is to set variables. The formula for calculating stochastics is as follows. For the purposes of illustration, we will use a 14-day stochastic. Note that two graph lines form the whole chart (see Figure 8-11).

The raw stochastic is defined as the position of today's close as a percentage of the range between the highest high and the lowest low for a defined time period (in this case, 14 days). The raw stochastic (*%K*) is smoothed exponentially to yield the *%D* value.

The calculations for the original or fast stochastic are the following:

For *%K*:

$$\%K = 100\,(C - L14)\,/\,(H14 - L14)$$

where C = the latest close, $L14$ is the lowest low for the time period, and $H14$ is the highest high .

For *%D*:

$$\%D = 100 \times (H9\,/\,L9)$$

where $H9$ is the 9-day sum of $C - L9$ and $L9$ is the 9-day sum of $H9 - L9$. The stochastic values are then smoothed with a simple moving average.

Assume that over the last 14 days the high in our market was 1274 and the low was 1232. In this example (see Figure 8-12), 1232 would have a stochastic value of 0; and 1253, which is the midpoint of the high and low, would have a stochastic value of 50. For the other line in the chart, the high, 1274, would have a stochastic value of 100; and 1253, which,

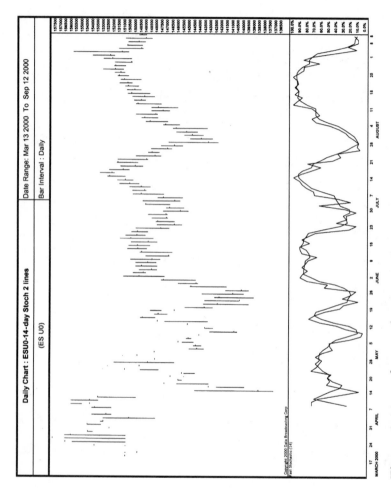

Figure 8-11 14-day Stochastic Dual Line

92

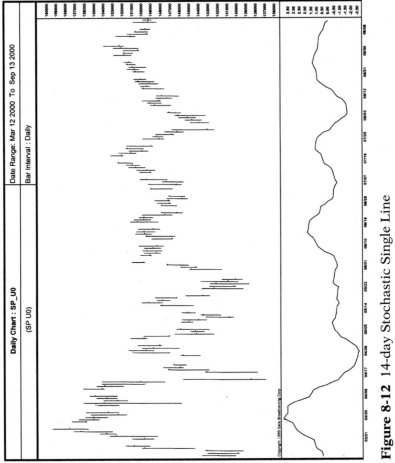

Figure 8-12 14-day Stochastic Single Line

as we have seen, is the midpoint of the high and low, would have a stochastic value of 50.

Mostly what you see when you are looking at a stochastic graphically are two lines that are smoothed and are being represented by %K and %D values. The smoothing of the data helps eliminate false signals. The raw stochastic is defined as the position of today's close as a percentage of the range between the highest high and the lowest low for a defined time period (in this case, 14 days). The raw stochastic (%K) is smoothed exponentially to yield the %D value.

To calculate the %K you take 2/3 of the previous %K and add 1/3 absolute value:

$$\%K = \frac{2}{3} pv\%K + \frac{1}{3} av\%K$$

To calculate the %D you take 2/3 the previous %D and add 1/3 %K:

$$\%D = \frac{2}{3} pv\%D + \frac{1}{3} av\%D$$

Consequently, the numbers are smoothed out by taking 2/3 of the previous values and then adding 1/3 new value in the above calculations.

Using Stochastics

You can use stochastics in many different ways. When they are used in conjunction with other indicators as a timing mechanism, stochastics can help to confirm good trades and, the hope is, filter out bad ones. If you trade in the direction of the stochastics, you can use certain values to determine buy and sell signals. The following are examples of a three-contract approach to buying and selling when the stochastics reach a certain price level. The following are examples of when you would buy and when you would sell based on this simple formula using the *%K* value.

BUY	SELL
Positive breakout stochastics above 25 percent, buy.	Close out position if stochastics go below 25 percent.
Add a position if stochastics go above 55 percent.	Close both positions if stochastics go below 50 percent.
Add a position if stochastics go above 70 percent.	Close all positions if stochastics go below 60 percent.
If stochastics go above 75 percent, add a position.	Close all positions if stochastics go below 75 percent.

SELL	BUY
Negative breakdown below 75 percent, sell one.	Close out positions if stochastics go above 75 percent.
Add a position if stochastics go below 45 percent.	Close both positions if stochastics go above 50 percent.

SELL	**BUY**
Add a position if stochastics go below 30 percent.	Close all positions if stochastics go above 40 percent.
If stochastics go below 25 percent, add a position.	Close all positions if stochastics go above 25 percent.

In both the scenarios set out in the preceding list, it is important to note that as a timing device and filter, stochastics can operate independently of other indicators to give you a simple approach to trading. However, it is always best to use stochastics in conjunction with other indicators to confirm what the stochastic indicators are telling you about the market. It is also important to consider the strength of the stochastic signals at any given time in any given market.

Signal Strength

You can use the signal strength, for instance, to help gauge a three-contract approach, adding contracts as the momentum in the market builds. Or you can use a one-contract approach, buying or selling only one contract at the second level. This would mean a one-contract approach would have a buy signal at 55 percent and a sell signal at 45 percent. By using these middle numbers for a one-contract approach you are filtering out many of the false signals that often occur at very high and very low stochastics. You are buying or selling only after a trend has developed and a high or low has been established. Although you may be eliminating some potentially good trades (because of your filtering), you are also filtering out some potentially bad trades. Don't approach this method with the attitude that you are going to miss a trade because of the filtering. The whole idea is to miss some trades. Over time, missing a proportionate number of bad trades will compensate for the missed good trades. What you are trying to accomplish is to optimize your overall trading, not just maximize the profits on a single trade. And most importantly, remember that there will always be another trade.

Relative Strength Index

The most popular and most misunderstood of all the oscillators is the relative strength index, or RSI. Developed by J. Welles Wilder, the RSI is calculated by determining an exponential average of upticks versus an average of downticks. As with all oscillators (except for momentum indicators), RSIs tend to lag the market by 1 to 5 days. This lagging makes them unaccountable as a timing mechanism. The RSI's real strengths lie in its ability to smooth out the sometimes choppy price charts and to provide you with values that can be used to determine if the markets are in an overbought or oversold condition. With RSIs it is as important to understand what you *are not* doing as it is to understand what you are doing. With a relative strength index you might expect that you are comparing two different markets or factors. You are not. In the case of an RSI you are comparing a single market's current strength with that of its own past performance.

In other words, you are seeking to determine how strong or weak the market is today compared with its strength or weakness during a particular past period. The past time period could be a few days or a few months. To calculate the RSI you must first determine the time period that you would like to use as your comparative basis. The shorter the time period used to calculate the RSI, the more sensitive the index will be and the wider (more comprehensive) its fluctuation will be. Because you want the oscillator to move to the wider extremes in order to receive overbought or oversold signals, you must use a somewhat shorter time period for your comparative analysis.

The two most common time periods are the 9-day and the 14-day interval. Although these periods are the most commonly used, you should experiment with other time frames in an effort to help improve your results. As with most technical indicators, many quote vendors (and virtually all analytic software providers) include a program for calculating the RSI with a simple series of keystrokes, so you don't really have to know the formula or how to do the calculations. Let's look at the calculations anyway so you will have a better understanding of the RSI function.

The 14-day RSI is calculated as follows:

$$RSI = \frac{100 \times RS}{1 + RS}$$

$$RS = \frac{\text{average of 14 days up closes}}{\text{average of 14 days down closes}}$$

To find the average up RS value, add the total number of points gained on up days for the past 14 days and then divide by 14. To find the down RS value, add the total number of points lost on down days for the past 14 days and then divide by 14. To use the RSI it should be plotted on a graph with a vertical scale between 0 and 100. When the RSI goes above 75, the market is considered overbought and you should refer to other timing indicators for confirmation of a decision to get out of a long position. Conversely, when the RSI goes below 25, you are in an oversold condition and you should consider getting out of short positions. Again, refer to other timing indicators for confirmation.

You must be judicious in your reliance on the RSI and understand that, by itself, it is almost never a reliable source for decision making. For instance, in a sharply rising or falling market, the overbought or oversold conditions to which the RSI points may not in and of themselves be good reasons to exit a trade. Simply because the RSI crosses over the 75 value or below the 25 value is not a reason to exit a profitable trade. In strong uptrends or downtrends where the market has strong momentum, simply moving above or below these values is not a good reason to get out of a trade and is definitely not a good reason to reverse one. A trend is a trend. And as we have emphasized with other oscillators, the RSI should only be used in conjunction with other indicators and should not be relied on to generate actual buy or sell signals.

Even though the RSI should not be used in isolation to generate signals, there are two instances in which the RSI indications have a greater value. The first instance is what is referred to as "RSI reversals," and the other instance is "RSI price divergences." In both these instances, the time frame for their use is limited and you should use other technical indicators for independent verification. In an uptrending market an RSI reversal formation occurs when the RSI value goes over 75 on one day and then crosses below 75 the next day. Conversely, in a bear market an RSI reversal formation occurs if the RSI goes below 25 one day and then crosses above 25 the next day. In both these instances you may have a true RSI reversal shaping up. Usually this reversal pattern represents what is best described as a short-term "blow-off" in the market.

These blow-offs may simply be 1-day spikes either up or down that do not indicate a reversal signal. So you need to use other technical indicators to confirm whether this RSI reversal formation represents a true reversal or is just a blip in an otherwise trending market. For instance, let's assume we are in a bull market. On a particular morning the market opens and trades sharply higher on a one-item news story (employment numbers, housing starts, purchasing managers' surveys, etc.). Then, later in the day, the market reverses with high volume and closes on the low. If this bull market is in the process of selling off and takes out the lows from the previous week, this could signal the possibility that the market has formed a major top. The auction process has tested the highs, the longs are covering, and there are fewer buyers at the higher levels.

The same scenario would hold true with a downside move early in a trading day followed by a breakout to the upside late in the day. This scenario could signal that a major bottom is being formed. Here, the market has auctioned downward, and there are no more sellers at the lower levels. Again, the key here is examining other indicators for verification of the RSI's trading signals.

RSI price divergence is another way in which the RSI can generate a buy or sell signal. In the case of an uptrend, the RSI will reach a lower high than its previous high and then turn lower while the actual market prices continue to go higher. Be careful not to get overly bearish in this situation. The first move into an overbought condition is generally an early warning signal, and it is not until the actual market price fails that you should take any action.

In the case of a downtrend, the RSI will reach a higher low than its previous low and then turn higher while the actual market prices continue to go lower. In this case, be careful not to get overly bullish. The first move into an oversold condition is generally an early warning signal, and it is not until the actual market price rallies that you should take any action.

CHAPTER
9

Moving Averages

L ike other indicators, moving averages assist in determining your trading strategy. However, using moving averages is like standing with one foot in a bucket of boiling water and the other foot in a bucket of ice water—on average you are fine. Separately, however, each foot has its own problem. This is an apt analogy when using moving averages. Moving averages can be very deceptive. Inexperienced traders can be easily deceived and should not be fooled by the simplicity of the concept: addition and short division. To calculate a 10-day moving average you add the market closing price of the last 10 days and divide by 10. Other types of averages include exponentially smoothed, weighted, and crossover methods and will be discussed also. But first (as with all indicators), it is important to understand how and why moving averages work, and why and when they do not work.

The good news is that of all the technical indicators, moving averages are probably the most widely used and easiest to understand. Moving averages work particularly well in trending markets. They can alert you to a developing trend and will also indicate when a trend is waning, has leveled out, or has reversed. Remember, however, that a moving average functions as a lagging indicator, not a leading indicator, and can only alert you that a trend has already begun, is intact, or is over. The moving average also acts as a smoothing device. By averaging the prices over a set number of days, a smoothing line is produced, making it easier to identify the underlying market trend. A shorter-term moving average, such as a 3-, 5-, or 10-day one, would conform to the market prices more closely than a 20- or a 40-day average. Shorter-term moving averages are much more reactive to price action than longer-term moving averages.

The general rule is that if you are only using moving averages to trade, which we *don't* recommend, shorter-term moving averages are probably more accurate. However, you will probably trade more often, and both your profits and your losses will be smaller. The opposite is true with longer-term moving averages. You will do fewer trades and generally have both larger profits and larger losses.

With longer-term moving averages when the markets are trending, you tend to give back much of your profits before you get a signal to get out. The longer-term moving average keeps you in trending markets and prevents whipsawing in and out of a position. But again, giving back profits after you realize (too late) that the trend is over can be frustrating.

With any simple moving average you are long the commodity if the market is above the moving average, and short if it is below. The trade is initiated either when the price crosses through the moving average or, in some cases, when the market closes above (see Figure 9-1) or below (see Figure 9-2) the moving averages. One of the issues to be considered with a simple moving average is that equal weight is given to each day's prices. For example, in a 10-day moving average, each day's price action is given a 10 percent weighting. Many analysts believe that more weight should be given to more recent price action and less to earlier. The reason for more weight on the most recent price action is that these analysts operate on the theory that older price action is not as relevant as current price action. A good fundamental example would be grains going up because of a drought, then it rains and market prices go down. If there is no more drought, the more recent price action should be more of a true indicator of market values.

The linearly weighted moving average was developed in an effort to control the weighting issue. In the example of a 10-day moving average, the last day added would be multiplied by 10, the previous day by 9, the day before that by 8, and so on. The total is then divided by the sum of the multipliers, which, in the case of the 10-day average, would be 55 (10+9+8+7+6+5+4+3+2+1=55). As in the case of all moving averages, the trick is to find an average that is quick enough to get you in or out of a trade, but slow enough to avoid whipsaws. The closer you look at simple moving averages, the clearer it becomes that you need another method to enhance the performances of both the shorter and longer averages. Thus we use filters. Filters are one of the calculations that technicians use to reduce the whipsawing and its corresponding profit repatriation. Some of the more popular filters are time filters, percentage bands, high and low bands, breakout filters, total-range filters, and percentage filters.

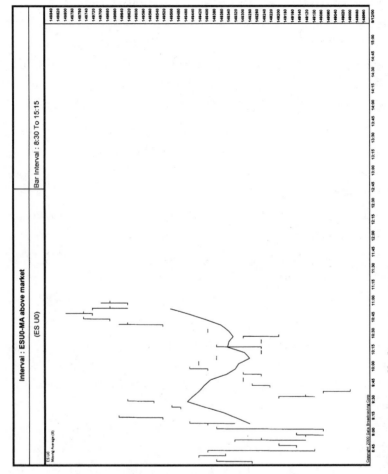

Figure 9-1 Bullish Moving Average

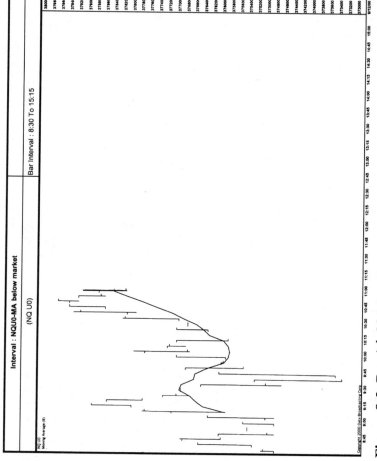

Figure 9-2 Bearish Moving Average

107

Time Filters

In order to be effective, time filters need a market that closes one or more days through the moving averages before a signal is generated. This attempts to filter out false signals based on the theory that most false signals tend to reverse themselves rather quickly.

Percentage Bands

Percentage bands also add a precautionary calculation to the moving average before the indicator generates a false signal. Percentage bands are calculated by plotting parallel lines a given percentage above and below the moving averages. A buy or sell signal would not be confirmed unless the market closed above or below the simple moving averages and above or below the bands.

High and Low Bands

High and low bands are developed by using the same time period for the bands that is used for the moving average. However, instead of using the closing prices, you use only the highs of the day for one calculation and the lows of the day for the other. High and low bands are also parallel lines plotted above and below the moving averages lines. A buy signal is generated when the market closes above the higher average and the lower line becomes your stop loss. A sell signal is generated when the market closes below the lower average and the higher average becomes your stop loss.

Breakout Filters

Breakout filters are signals that require something other than a moving average to generate a trading signal. Many different types of systems can generate breakout signals when used in conjunction with moving averages. These filters will help to eliminate being consistently whipsawed in a short-term trading range. Breakouts on weekly charts, point and figure charts, market profile indicators, and many other momentum-based indicators will help confirm the validity of an impending trend. You might use a breakout filter, for example, after you get a moving average–generated buy signal. You wait until the prices go above the highs of the last 10 days. This 10-day breakout can be used to confirm the moving average buy signal. If the market does not go above the highs of the last 10 days, it is possible that you have a trading range market and the breakout filter kept you from buying at the highs.

Total-Range Filters

Total-range filters are very simple and require only that the entire daily trading range of the commodity from high to low be above or below the moving average in order to generate a trading signal.

Percentage Filters

Percentage filters require that the market close above or below the moving average plus an additional percentage of the range or by an established number of points above or below the moving average. For example, one manner in which to structure a percentage filter would be take the moving average of 50 and add or subtract a percentage from that number. If your percentage was 10 percent, then the market would have to be above 55 or below 45 in order to generate a buy or sell signal.

It is important to keep in mind that filters are not guarantees; they are merely artificial calculations, mathematical constructs, employed to confirm a buy or sell signal. You can change filters as your view of the market changes and as your familiarity with the filters increases with experience. With experience you will very quickly learn that filters create their own dilemma because of their inherent limitations. Fewer limits placed on the filter will result in fewer protections and a greater number of potentially false signals. Conversely, the larger or more expansive the filter, the greater the likelihood of generating a higher percentage of delayed signals. Delayed signals will result in late entry or exit points. To help verify signals and make moving averages and filters more effective, you can use different techniques (or methods) to increase confirmations. A double-crossover method that uses multiple averages to generate a buy or sell is often used.

The Double-Crossover Method

The double-crossover method produces a buy or a sell signal when the shorter-term moving average crosses through a longer-term moving average. An example of a double-crossover buy signal is when a 10-day moving average crosses above a 30-day moving average (see Figure 9-3). Conversely, a sell signal is generated when a 10-day moving average crosses below a 30-day moving average (see Figure 9-4). The time differences between the moving averages, 10 days and 30 days, are not individually the critical factors in generating the trading signal. These are artificial time factors that you impose. The critical factor for this method of confirmation is the action of the shorter-term moving average crossing over the longer-term moving average. By using two moving averages together, your trading signals will lag the market more than they would if you used a single moving average. By using the two moving averages together, however, your approach to the market will produce fewer whipsaws.

The Triple-Crossover Method

The triple-crossover method is based on the theory that if two moving averages are better than one, then three moving averages must be better than two. It does not hold true, however, that four moving averages are better than three! The most popular three numbers used in formulating the triple-crossover confirmation are the 4-9-18 day moving averages. To use these three moving averages to define and confirm a trend in a bull market you would need to have the 4-day average close above the 9-day average, which in turn closes above the 18-day average (see Figure 9-5). For confirmation of a bear market using the three numbers, their effect is reversed—the 4-day average closes under the 9-day average, which in turn closes under the 18-day average (see Figure 9-6).

A buy alert occurs when the 4-day average goes above both the 9- and 18-day average. This is the initial buy signal; the

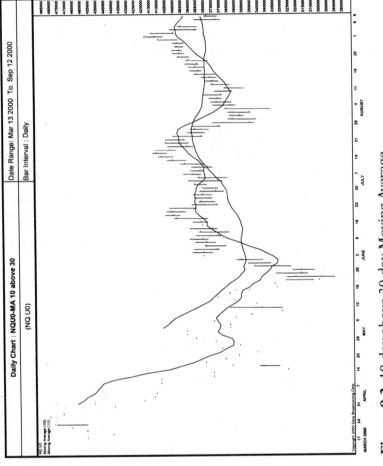

Figure 9-3 10-day above 30-day Moving Average

112

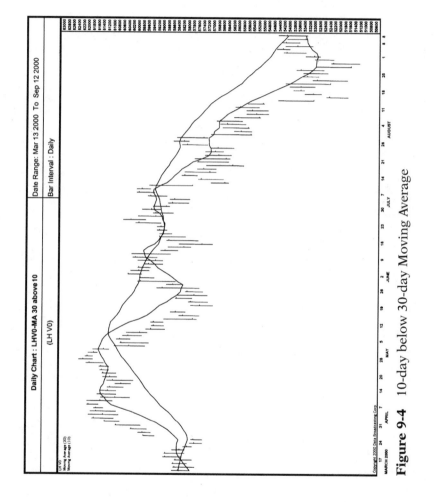

Figure 9-4 10-day below 30-day Moving Average

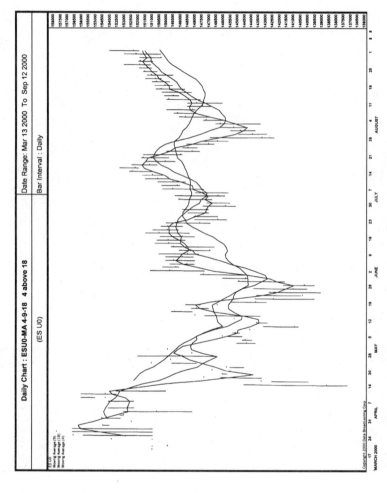

Figure 9-5 4-day above 9/18-day Moving Average

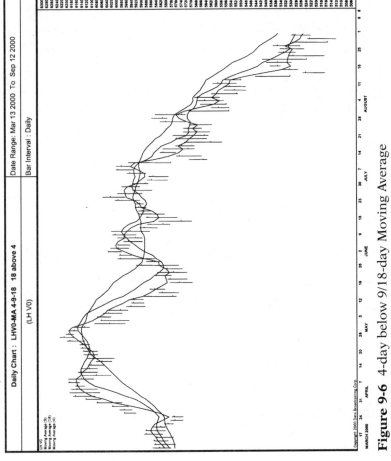

Figure 9-6 4-day below 9/18-day Moving Average

confirmation occurs when the 9-day average also goes above the 18-day average. When all moving averages are in proper alignment, the 4-, 9-, and 18-day moving averages will parallel each other. Many times in an uptrend, the averages will make a correction, and the averages will become intermingled. An upward trend could be interrupted for a period of time and go sideways, or it could come to an abrupt end when this occurs. In either case, use this as a signal of caution and be ready to get out if necessary. Many traders use these mixed signals to get out of their positions; others, however, use the signals as an opportunity to add to their positions. Experience and market knowledge will help you determine how you react to intermingled signals.

Rubber Band Theory

Often, in an uptrending or downtrending market, the market prices will move away from the moving averages by a considerable number of points, creating what appears to be overbought or oversold conditions. To form a mental picture of this, imagine a rubber band fastened to both the market price movement and the moving average fluctuation. The tension on the rubber band, when it is stretched, limits the market's ability to continue its move without some corresponding shift in momentum or retracement. In order to get confirmation for your buy or sell signals in a rubber band scenario, you should rely on other indicators for timing the retracement, such as stochastics and volume. If you get a low-volume retracement compared with your moving average and a signal from your stochastics, the timing for your purchase or sale is confirmed.

CHAPTER

10

Volume and Open Interest

Volume and open interest are the primary indicators upon which most traders rely to confirm that a trend has begun or is over. Rising and falling volume and open interest, especially near the tops or bottoms of a market, can alert you to the potential for a major top or bottom. Many traders will ignore volume and open interest when doing pure technical analysis. But ignoring these two market characteristics is not always prudent and can give you a one-dimensional view of the market. We have found that by including volume and open interest as part of tracking the price action, you will sometimes see important turning points taking shape in the market. By ignoring volume and open interest and just following price action, you are looking at the market in one dimension and do not have sufficient depth in your analysis to make a properly calculated trade.

Volume and open interest offer you an insight into what larger traders are doing. The conventional wisdom is that most large traders, commercial and institutional accounts, tend to know what they are doing more often than the smaller retail traders. Although this is not axiomatic, it is a fairly good indication of activity. Knowing when the larger traders enter and exit the market is valuable information, and volume and open interest are good indicators of that information.

Volume

Volume is defined as the total number of contracts traded in a specified time period. Most traders usually track the volume of the most active month of an individual commodity on a daily basis. You can also plot volume for a longer or shorter period of time, such as hourly or weekly, depending on your system requirements and the perspective you are working to achieve. Volume, as represented in Figure 10-1, is plotted by a vertical bar located at the bottom of the bar chart under the specific day's price action. Volume in the futures markets is represented as a net number, a summary of round turns.

For instance, if 200 people bought a particular contract and 200 people sold that same contract, the volume would be 200. If both the longs and the shorts were added together, the resulting number would be inflated. Thus, a buyer and a seller result in a one-contract transaction. It is also important to remember that volume and open-interest figures are reported a day late in the commodity markets. The current day's figure is an estimated figure and is not confirmed until the actual figures are released the following day.

Open Interest

Open interest reflects the total number of open contracts (unliquidated) as of the close of the trading day. Unlike volume, where the total number of buyers and sellers is netted, open interest calculates the number of unliquidated long and short positions that traders are carrying in their accounts (see Figure 10-2). Following the same example as we did with volume where 200 people bought the market and 200 people sold it, open interest calculates how many of those 200 buy and sell contracts remain open as of the close. If 100 of the buyers and 100 of the sellers were initiating a new position, and another 100 buyers and 100 sellers were getting out or liquidating a contract, then the open interest would remain unchanged. Using the same example, if 150 of the buyers and 150 of the sellers were initiating a new position and the other 50 buyers and 50 sellers were getting out of or liquidating a contract, then the open interest would go up by 100. Conversely, if 50 of the buyers and 50 of the sellers were initiating new positions and the other 150 buyers and 150 sellers were getting out of or liquidating a contract, then the open interest would decrease by 100.

To summarize, if both traders are initiating a new position, open interest will go up. If both traders are liquidating an existing position, open interest will go down. If one trader is initiating a new trade and the other is liquidating an existing trade, open interest will remain unchanged. Remember, divide the total number of buyers and sellers by 2, because it takes a buyer and a seller to create one contract. Open interest is plotted using a horizontal line located above the volume figures and below the specific daily bar. The open interest is the total number of open contracts of both the buyers and sellers divided by 2.

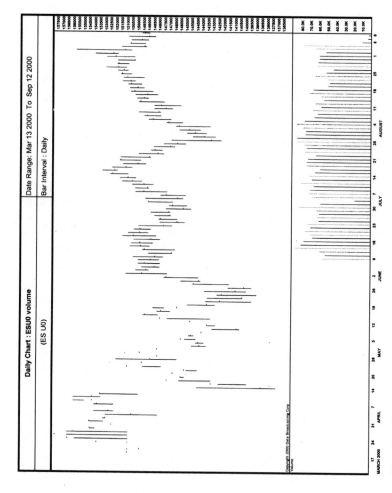

Figure 10-1 Volume

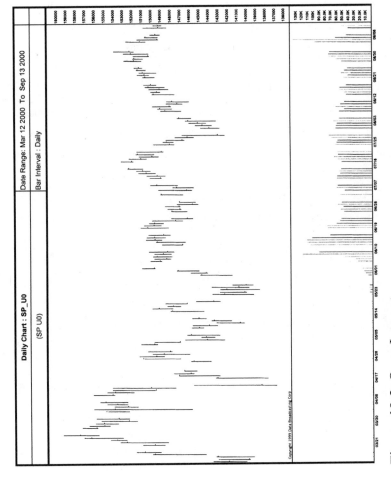

Figure 10-2 Open Interest

The change in open interest is based on either an increase or decrease from the previous day's open interest. When plotting increases and decreases in open interest, one should remember that just like price action, open interest works in seasonal cycles. For example, you could expect to see an increase in open interest in the winter months on commodities that are sensitive to cold weather, such as heating oil or orange juice. In the spring and fall, you will see an increase in open interest in the grain markets, as farmers will be planting and harvesting in those seasons and must hedge their crops. So before you calculate any increases or decreases in open interest, be sure to adjust your figures for the seasonal tendencies of that specific commodity.

Also remember that when a fundamental situation occurs in the market, such as flooding or drought, you can expect to see large increases in both the open interest and volume. Large increases in both the open interest and volume will lead to sharp price increases because money is flowing into the market. By looking at the percentage of increase in volume and open interest, you can gauge the possible strength of the current price trend. For example, when volume and open interest are rising, you could expect to see the trend continue in its current direction. If, on the other hand, you see declining volume and open interest, you can interpret this as a sign that the current price trend could be exhausted.

Interpreting Volume

Think of high volume as increasing the intensity or momentum of the market. The heavier the volume, the more intensity or momentum the market will have. High volume can also be used to confirm price action. Volume should rise or expand in the direction of the existing price trend. In a bull, or rising market, volume should increase when the market is going up and decrease when the market has setbacks. It is these quiet or low-volume days when profit taking drives the market and it drops back to a level of support. At the support level on days such as this, you should be initiating new long positions or adding to existing long positions.

If, however, you see volume start to increase on a decline in a bull market, this increase in volume could be signaling that the upward trend could be ending. Unlike some other technical indicators, volume is actually a leading indicator in that it precedes price action. When you see a lack of volume in the market, traders are not putting pressure on the market. You will notice this lack of pressure in the volume figures before you see a reversal of price action. Because of this leading action, many traders keep a close eye on volume at all times.

There is one volume scenario of which you must be aware, and that is a key reversal, or high-volume blow-off. Under normal circumstances, when a market is at a historically high or low point it is susceptible to the possibility of a key reversal, or high-volume blow-off. In a bull market, if an extremely bullish news story comes across the wire, every trader and his broker will be buying, causing the market to go sharply higher. If, however, during the trading day the market cannot hold the price gains achieved earlier, sellers will enter the market, forcing recent buyers to sell and the old buyers to take profits on their long positions. From the trader's perspective, this reversal confirms that the bullish news has been factored into the auction process. Subsequent news will be neutral or bearish. In either case the news will drive the market lower.

A key reversal, or a high-volume blow-off, generally occurs after a sustained rise or fall in the market, a news story that moves prices further in the direction of the trend, or volume that is two to five times more than normal. To establish a new position on the assumption that a key reversal, or blow-off, has taken place, you would enter a stop order at "unchanged on the day" in order to stop yourself into a new long or short position. If, for instance, the market trend is up and the market is sharply higher in the morning because of a news story, place a sell stop at unchanged. If the market sells off below unchanged, you will be short. The opposite holds true for a falling market. Be aware that if by the end of the day you have a profit in your position, protect it. If not, get out on the close. A true key reversal, or blow-off, will close at the opposite extreme of the day. If the market closes in the middle of the daily trading range or if you have a loss in your position, exit immediately because it is not a true key reversal, or blow-off.

Interpreting Open Interest

Many of the volume concepts also apply to open interest. Remember, rising volume and increasing open interest in an uptrend is bullish and in a downtrend is bearish. In an uptrend, money is flowing into the market; and in a downtrend, money is flowing out of the market. In both instances, prices must adjust accordingly. However, in a rising market if you start to see a loss of open interest, you are seeing short covering. The shorts buying their way out of losing positions cause such a rally. In this instance, the market goes higher because the shorts are covering, but the open interest goes down because their buying is a liquidation of open positions. This short covering is bearish because no new longs are getting in and the uptrend will probably dissipate once the short covering is over.

The opposite is true in a downtrend. With rising open interest, new money is moving into the market, reflecting new short selling, so the trend lower should continue and is therefore bearish. However, if both price and open interest are declining, the longs are selling their losing positions, causing open interest to go lower. This is bullish because no new shorts are entering the market and the downtrend will probably dissipate once the losing longs liquidate their positions. Keep a close eye on open interest toward the end of a major market move. When you see rising open interest throughout the price trend and then a leveling off or decline, take this as an early warning that the trend may change.

If you see extremely high open interest at the top of a market followed by a sudden price decline, take warning. You could be in for a sharp and violent fall in the market. Traders who got long at the market highs now have losing positions and will be forced to liquidate those positions, which will add to the selling pressure and intensify the new price decline. Think of high open interest as a lead weight tied to your feet. It does not mean you cannot jump higher, but the lead weight will certainly make it harder. In other words, all the new buyers are already in the market; there are no new buyers to drive the market higher.

If you see open interest increase during a sideways market or during a period of consolidation, expect the market to make an extended move in the direction in which it breaks out. In a consolidation period or sideways market, nobody knows which way the market is going to go. However, many traders are establishing new positions in anticipation of an ensuing trend. When the market finally breaks out, half of the traders in the market will be wrong and will have to cover their losing positions, which will increase the momentum of the market. When the market breaks out, those on the wrong side will react immediately, causing the reaction to be both quick and sharp. If you figure that half of the people have losing positions after the market breaks out, you can see why the higher the open interest, the greater the chance for a substantial price move.

Commitment-of-Traders Report

Once a month the Commodity Futures Trading Commission releases a report detailing the open-interest statistics for the previous month. This report is divided into three categories: large hedgers, large speculators, and small speculators. By regulation, larger traders must disclose their cumulative positions if they are at or above reportable levels. Each market has open-interest levels that traders cannot exceed. These levels are established by the CFTC, and any open interest not reported is attributed to small traders.

As mentioned earlier, conventional wisdom dictates that large traders are usually considered to be the "smarter money" as opposed to the smaller, less informed, and less skillful individual retail trader. The same conventional wisdom holds that the smaller trader will lose money and leave the market. So the "experts" tend to follow the larger traders on the assumption that they are the most successful. If the large trader report shows large hedgers and large speculators heavily long and small traders heavily short, the market has a bullish potential.

There are two disadvantages of trying to trade based on this report. First, it is 2 weeks old, and, second, there could be a sudden fundamental change in the market which forces all the large hedgers and large speculators to liquidate and reverse their positions. Such a large and sudden shift would have a dramatic effect on market prices because of the large volume entering the market in the same direction in a short period of time. Generally, however, the report offers a good look at where the smart money thought the market was going in the previous month. In months where there is some adverse fundamental situation, such as weather, this report can help verify whether it is just media hype or if the smart money, especially the large hedgers who are most affected, believes that the fundamental situation is real.

Defining Trending and Cyclical Markets

If each of us had a crystal ball, we would get out of sideways markets before they retraced and stay with trending markets as long as possible. Since we don't have a crystal ball, we need indicators to help us determine whether a market is trending. The salient characteristic of most agricultural markets is that they are cyclical. In other words, they move back and forth in a fairly well-defined channel of support and resistance. To explain this phenomenon, let's examine the different products in the meat markets and see why they tend to be fairly cyclical markets. The meat complex is made up of feeder cattle, live cattle, live hogs, pork bellies, and chicken.

In the absence of fundamental news like severe winter weather or a drought in summer, the supply-demand curve is fairly predictable. From the supply side we know, for example, approximately how many cattle or hogs will be produced in a specific month. We also know from the demand side, barring any unusual major meat promotion, approximately how much meat is going to be consumed in an average month. Imagine walking into a supermarket each month and looking at the price of bacon. On months when you see the price of bacon at $1.50 to $2.50 per pound, you will buy bacon. When bacon is priced between $2.50 and $5.00 per pound, you leave bacon out of your shopping cart. As the old saying goes, "Nothing cures high prices like high prices." By not purchasing bacon you decrease demand for that product while increasing demand for a less expensive cut or an altogether different meat.

As demand is tempered by higher prices, consumers switch to other cuts of meats and support those products until they reach their point of price resistance. This same scenario occurs in most agricultural markets, where the consumer switches to alternative products based on price. When we look at characteristics of trending markets, there is generally a need to buy or sell that market and hold the position for a while.

The three best trending groups of markets are all related in the sense that they are all financially oriented: stock indexes, foreign currencies, and interest rates. Generally with this group of markets, overwhelming fundamental factors will cause a prolonged trend to develop. In times of inflation you can count on the Fed to raise interest rates in order to slow down the rate of inflation (or even when there is no inflation, to cool down the stock market). During inflationary periods, the inflation tends to feed on itself and worsen for a substantial period of time. Likewise, interest rates, which are used to combat inflation, will continue to rise for an almost equal length of time. Once a country's interest rate policy is in place, it tends to defend that current policy and not flip-flop. Consistency in government policy is essential to maintain confidence. Foreign currencies represent another area where government policies (whether or not driven by an external body such as the IMF) set the tone for a prolonged trend in a particular currency. There are also fundamental factors within countries that will cause a currency to fluctuate.

The monetary and fiscal policies of governments determine the direction of the economy. Controlling the money supply and spending affects all sectors of an economy. Once those policies are in place, it's hard for an administration to change. Governments must show confidence in the direction of their decisions or face the uncertainty of a lack of confidence. A lack of confidence in policy is virtually the same as bad policy. Either one would have a weakening effect on a nation's currency. Just as negative news can weaken a currency, positive news will strengthen the currency. Absent some compelling event, once a trend gets started in a specific country, that trend tends to continue for a prolonged period, and the effect on that particular currency is prolonged as well. Needless to say, currencies have "come under attack." These instances are anomalies and do not fit the general trend profile.

The stock market is an excellent example of a long-term trending market. Since 1984 the stock market has experienced one of the largest bull markets in history. Several major fundamental factors are at play in the stock market, and those fundamental factors should stay in place until the years 2006 to 2008. The highest percentage of baby boomers and immigrants will reach their peak spending periods between 1995 and 2008. Computers and the Internet have swept us into the beginning of an "information and technology age." Productivity and consumer confidence are high, and unemployment and interest rates are low.

By looking at the predictable spending patterns of the U.S. population, coupled with a full array of all the new products, services, and ways to buy them, our economy and our stock market should be on an upward trend until at least 2006–2008. As we move this new crop of baby boomers and immigrants through our economy, we see predictable spending patterns at each age. When you are just out of school, earnings and spending are low, but savings are high. With marriage and a first house, spending starts to rise. Next, add children and a larger house with more furniture, and spending continues to rise. Finally, there's one last burst of spending as the children go to college. Then spending starts to decline as you enjoy what you have not had time to before. So from the age of 21, the beginning of your own independent spending, until your children graduate from college when you are 47–55, you have an accelerating, predictable spending pattern. This pattern will help to define long-term trends, but it is disconnected from short-term swings and connections.

We have noticed that some technicians will only take trading signals in the direction of the fundamental trend. For example, we have been following one of our more successful S&P position traders, and in the past 3 years he has been either long or out of the market, never short. He believes the market is going sharply higher and except for temporary setbacks, the money to be made in trend following will come from buying the S&Ps, not selling them.

It's convenient to have a major fundamental factor, such as demographic-driven spending, that you can use as a benchmark, because you can quantify it and develop a technical formula. But before you start investing your money based on general fundamental factors, it would be wise to also develop a technical formula to verify your potential results. We have reviewed several indicators and their calculations that can give you a good idea of when a new trend is going to develop. One such calculation can help you formulate where the support and resistance levels are going to be. This calculation covers a relatively short period of 9 to 14 days.

Determining Support and Resistance Levels

First solve for X, which is an anticipated price based on weighting the most recent close more heavily than the average close for the period. This is expressed by

$$X = (H + L + C + C) / 4$$

where H is the highest close in the period, L is the lowest close, and C is the most recent close.

Let's say $H = 1250$, $L = 1230$, and $C = 1232$. Then

$$X = \frac{1250 + 1230 + 1232 + 1232}{4} = \frac{4944}{4} = 1236$$

Now, you can calculate high resistance and low support:

$$\text{High resistance} = X + H - L$$

$$\text{Low support} = X + L - H$$

or

$$\text{High resistance} = 1236 + 1250 - 1230 = 1256$$

$$\text{Low support}\;\; = 1236 + 1230 - 1250 = 1216$$

Based on this formula, we have determined that the market will run into resistance at 1256 and find support at 1216. If the market reaches either the support or resistance levels on low volume, be careful. You want to see heavy volume when it goes above or below the support or resistance areas as a confirmation that the market has indeed broken out. When the market goes beyond the high resistance level, it is a sign to go long and ride with the trend. Likewise, when a high-volume market breaks through the low support level, it is time to be short.

Money Management Techniques

If you are trading systems or methodologies, your approach will be organized to provide you with proper risk and reward formulas for each individual trade. When you consider a diverse portfolio of trades, however, the picture becomes a little less clear. To bring clarity to this picture, there are well-reasoned money management guidelines that you should learn and apply. Some of the items to be considered in money management include contract liquidity, margin requirements, percentage of risk, and contract volatility. Diversification, of course, is the primary and organizing principle behind all good money management, and to be diversified in trending markets is the best of all worlds.

Money is made in trends, and by diversifying into trending

markets you increase your odds for success. Diversification is important, because when you are dealing with longer-term, trending, noncorrelating markets, the markets should be trending in your direction most of the time except for an occasional round of profit taking.

Diversification reduces the drama and the trauma that correlation can inflict on your portfolio. If all your money were in correlated markets, the highs would be higher but the lows would be even lower. Diversification gives you a tighter channel between your largest overall profit and largest drawdown. You should plot your portfolio's performance on a graph and apply the same technical analysis to it as you would apply to the markets. In this way you can trade your overall equity curve. In sideways or nontrending markets, how much of your equity falls below or rises above your moving averages will give you a sense of the boundaries within which your system operates when the markets are trending and when they are not. When the markets are trending at the highest end of your historical highs, it is a good idea to fine-tune your exit procedures to capture the most profit. Based on historical performance, your winning streak is near an end, but don't get out until the markets tell you to based on your technical indicators.

Realizing you are near one of your historical highs and planning your exit will help you avoid the psychological pitfall of being euphoric. By avoiding the euphoric belief that you know more than either the market or your system does, you do not buy more contracts at what is the potential high for the move. If you buy more contracts because of your euphoric belief, you risk having to carry those extra contracts as the market falls. Carrying extra contracts from the high of your profit channel to the low of your drawdown channel should be avoided at all costs since the compounding effect will cause your drawdown channel to increase because of the additional contracts.

Example: If you have two contracts and you add a third at the highs, your drawdown potential is 33 percent greater. By defining and acknowledging the profit and drawdown channels, you have taken away the possibility of being duped into a feeling of safety, and you have prepared yourself for a timely exit.

Margin Requirements

Allocating capital for margin requirements in a diversified portfolio will determine the appropriate number of contracts for each trade within the portfolio. In keeping with a diversified approach, it is prudent not to allocate more than 25 percent of your working capital to any one sector at any given time. In assessing the capital available for margin you must consider the effect of leverage and make appropriate adjustments for market movements. For instance, assuming your account is $100,000, you would want to restrict your margin allocation to $50,000 and hold $50,000 in available margin excess over and above any excess available from the other $50,000. You should further allocate the available $50,000 so you have no more than $12,500 committed to any one group of correlated markets.

Even with correlated markets, however, there are exceptions. Consider the following example, where you have one position in a sector net opposite the other positions in the sector. Assume that you are long soybeans, wheat, and corn, and that the cumulative margin requirements for the positions are $12,500 (your maximum allocation for that sector). You can take a sell signal for bean oil. By taking the short position in the same complex, depending on the market conditions, you can position yourself for a move based on the activity in other markets. Although the soybean market might be strong, other bean products such as oil and meal might be weak because of competition from other oils such as coconut or corn.

We see this structure in the crush and the reverse crush spread within the soybean complex. Soybean processors buy soybeans and crush them into two products, oil and meal, and then sell those products to food processors. This market process is continuous, and the supply and demand factors affecting the different products are constantly being adjusted. An imbalance in any given area of either supply or demand can present good opportunities to take contrary positions.

Dollar Units

The $50,000 available margin (net the excess) should be further broken down into dollar units as opposed to number of commodities. Divide the dollar amount by 40, which in our example would be $50,000 divided by 40, or $1250 per unit. Never risk more than 2 units on any single trade or 10 units (25 percent) on any correlated sector. Thus as an automatic filter you will not take any trade that gives you a $2500 or more risk. Does this mean if you only have a $1250 risk you can do two contracts? In theory, yes, providing other factors are in place such as a strong buy or sell signal. By doing this you are weighing trades based on risk at equal values. However, say you were to buy one S&P 500 contract and one corn contract. They certainly do not have equal values. If we determine number of contracts based solely on margin requirements, as opposed to risk, our risk would be too high.

Example: Assume the S&P 500 has a margin of $24,700; corn has a margin requirements of $540. Does this mean that for every 1 contract of the S&P 500 you do, you should do 45 corn contracts? No, you cannot risk more than $2500 per unit trade, so you would only be able to risk $50 per contract, or the equivalent of a 1 cent stop, a sure loser.

By calculating the number of contracts based on risk, you allow both the maximum risk and profit potential on each trade. Using the same example, if you were risking 10 cents or $500 on each corn contract, you could do five corn contracts with a risk of $500 each and it is the same risk as one S&P 500 contract with a $2500 risk.

Contract Liquidity

Contract liquidity (or the lack of it) is an important factor in determining the spread between the bid and offer. That point spread is crucial, because you buy at the bid and sell at the offer. The wider the spread, the more it costs you to get in and out of the markets.

Example: Suppose you are trading bonds and the bid is 116.21 and the offer is 116.22. There is a 1-point spread, or $31.25. That is a liquid market. An example of an illiquid market is pork bellies. The bid could be 4050 and the offer 4075. That's a 25-point spread, or $100. In addition to the difference between the bid and the offer, you can have a problem getting out of the market if it locks limit. Most commodity contracts have a daily price limit, which is the maximum they are allowed to move. If a report comes out in pork bellies showing that a promotion of bacon cheeseburgers by a large fast-food restaurant has created much more demand than the available supply, the market could go several days at the daily limits without trading. So what started out to be a $1000 risk has suddenly turned into a $5000 losing trade.

This is not to say you should not trade in markets with less liquidity, because there are certainly opportunities, but just tread lightly.

Self-Discipline

Self-discipline in applying money management principles is like self-discipline in anything else—either you have it and you reap its benefits, or you do not and you suffer the consequences. Constantly monitoring the ever-changing risk landscape is critical. A risk-controller friend of mine once said, "Risk problems are always out there. They're just lurking below the surface." As the garage attendant at the Chicago Mercantile Exchange explained to us once, "The cars stay the same; only the drivers change." Many money management programs are available, but none produces better results than limiting your risk in a simple manner and giving yourself the most possible profit potential. Remember the old adage that advises that the way we do one thing is the way we do everything.

The Voice of the Leaders in Futures and Electronic Trading

The growth of electronic futures trading did not just happen overnight. In nearly all cases it required individuals with a sensitivity to customer needs as well as technical knowledge and foresight regarding the direction of the industry. The best way to understand what was involved in this electronic revolution is to hear from the major players.

The interviews on the following pages cover a range of opinions representing the FCMs, the exchanges, the floor traders, and industry leaders. By reading their words regarding electronic futures trading, you can get a sense of the passion, attitudes, and goals of these industry leaders.

Interview with Glenn Susz

Glenn Susz is the IT manager and developer of the software and systems for LeoWeb, one of the pioneering FCM systems in utilizing electronics and trading platforms that were accessible to customers.

Q. Other than purely technical issues, what roadblocks did you face and, alternately, in what areas did you make quick progress in dealing with the company?

A. Actually, it was a combination of things. One of them was always the vision and understanding that the business was moving in a certain direction and that Internet-based trading was the future. Just like with the web sites. Initially the company didn't want to put money into one. "What do we need a web site for?" They had that same mentality regarding electronic trading. "Who's going to want to do that?" And so getting somebody to believe in it, and then take on the cause to be a backer within the organization, was difficult. That was one big block. The other was since LeoWeb was not a revenue center, it was always hard to get either the funding or time from people. They had day-to-day crises, and they were concerned about the bottom line. So this was a project that was always a year off. It was up and coming, and it provided a really small amount of revenue, if any, so for them it was just a sinkhole.

Q. Did they lose money on this at the beginning?

A. Absolutely. The hardware and the start-up costs for the lines, routers, connections, and other items were quite an investment. This was true when LEO was a dial-up system, when we were on the bulletin board, all the way up and through the Internet phase. With every change in technology there was new hardware to be purchased. The other costs, because we were ahead of the curve, were also expensive because tools weren't available. Now you can go out and buy off-the-shelf administrative software. We had to write certain programs that now you can buy off the shelf for $39.95 or get as shareware, such as automatic scheduling programs or automatic backup software, things of that nature. We had to write a lot of administrative utilities ourselves. Going along that same line, there was the cost associated with upgrades. The costs of upgrades were always hidden from users as Microsoft progressed from Windows 3.1, to Windows 95, then Windows 98, and now Office 2000. Each of those upgrades caused concerns for compatibility problems.

We had to rewrite programs, do things differently, or just test all the implementations and permutations of that software. Does the upgrade work on this machine or that machine? Those tests are expensive also. The tests provided no income or benefits, but they had to be done. It's one thing to ask somebody for a thousand dollars so we could make this software do something better—that is a good investment you can rationalize. For that thousand dollars I can get more out of the software. But in our case, we had to say give me a thousand dollars, because I have to see if it's going to work next week on Office 2000, and it is still going to be the exact program you need. We are going to test the software and hope that we are still exactly where we are today with no improvements and no benefits. So it was always a battle to make them understand and to get the funding for all aspects of the development.

Q. I know when I first saw the Internet back in 1995, the Internet really was not used by many people except for those in colleges and certain government facilities. When I discovered what e-mail could do and how costs could be cut, one of my first thoughts was we are spending a lot of money on faxes and we can accomplish the same thing for literally a thousandth of that cost. The potential benefits of the Internet seemed too good to be true. Being in the commodity business, sometimes you see a trading program that seems too good to be true, and it usually is. In this case, certainly, that's wrong. It turned out that the Internet is not only all what we thought it would be, but probably much, much more. Did you find any of the resistance you got was because what was being offered by the Internet seemed too good to be true?

A. Absolutely. I came from O'Connor Associates, an option-trading firm, which was pretty advanced at the time, so in 1987–1989 we were already doing things over the Internet. We were dealing a lot with universities, and we were communicating with them via e-mail. Also at that time, all the client servers were using the TCP/IP and that's what the Internet uses, so we were using that type of design already in the trading systems. Not everyone was used to that system. We had to say, "I know you are used to doing things this way" (and they did everything with dial-up networks and file servers), and to bring them over to the client server mentality was a hurdle. Same thing now with the Internet. We say, "I know you are used to dial-up modems and lease lines, but now you have the Internet," and so we are back to the same hurdle: Who's going to use it? Only schools and universities or government contractors have the Internet connection. The farmer is not going to have an Internet connection.

Knowing that it would take time for the Internet to progress throughout society, we had to ask ourselves, are we going to develop the software now so that we are ready when it is out there, or are we going to wait until it's out there and then start developing the software? It was a battle to convince management to do this now. As more and more people used the software, it would become more and more cost-effective for the firm. But first things first, just like e-mail. Now we send statements via e-mail, and at first it was to a very small percentage of clients. The company took advantage of that, yet it took time, energy, and money to design and write those systems to take the equity runs and send them out via e-mail. But now clients demand that service. It increases every day.

Q. Do you think people were concerned because of the unknown aspect of computers at the time?

A. From the customer's perspective it was new technology, and people are afraid of change. The customer says, "I always got it over the fax," or "I always called my broker." The fact was that the technology existed, and regardless of how stable it was, the customers did not want more change.

Some brokers and introducing brokers had computers, but they used DOS. So getting them to buy a color monitor and a mouse for Windows, because they had to be able to point and click, represented a change. Everything was being written for Windows. They had to have it. Getting people to change was a challenge, especially when their mentality was, "I have my hundred customers. I'm doing it this way. I am happy. I don't want to change." Once they did change though, we then had to deal with the end user, the customer. With the customer, there was a fear factor with many questions. Is it safe? What if it breaks? What if somebody comes and steals my information? What if somebody else can see this information? The media had hyped the security issue of hackers and snoopers on the Web. Yes, it's a possibility that you could sniff stuff over the Internet. If a person is that smart and capable, and has the mentality of a criminal, wouldn't the person be better off going after an ATM or a bank as opposed to trying to sniff Bill's statements? So we had to overcome the media-created fear factor of the Internet.

Q. All anyone (a hacker) could do is enter a trade. The person couldn't profit from it, could he?

A. No, it would be difficult to profit from it. The other thing is that having those packets of information doesn't mean you can decipher it. In most cases it's a string of numbers and things. It's not just a program that formats and looks readable. It gives what your total equity is and everything else. You may just see a string of numbers, and trying to determine the date as opposed to the dollar amount could be meaningless in that packet unless somebody really knows what he's looking for. It's easier to walk into this place and just take something off a desk than it is to go and sniff it over the Internet. You give your credit card to a dollar-an-hour clerk at a gas station and that's okay, but you won't use a 128-bit encryption over the Internet to buy something from Sharper Image. You'll go to a restaurant and give your credit card to a waitress who smiles and says thank you and is gone for a half an hour while you finish your drink and comes back and she keeps your carbons and that's okay, but you won't use 128-bit encryption over the Internet. So it's that fear factor we're still seeing in the trading world. The "what ifs" could go on forever.

Q. Since clients are entering their own orders without a broker, what about risk control?

A. How do we control the risk now on the systems? Can the person place this trade or not? Does the person have enough margin to be able to place the trade? The current system over the phones is that someone calls up and says, "Hi, this is Joe Blow. Buy me two Dec S&Ps for account ABC," and the clerk says OK and does it. Then at the 4:00 prelim or equity run they realize, "Oh, we gotta call Bill back and tell him to get out of this position." That's the risk in the real world, but suddenly because it's electronic, we are forced to believe that it has to be the real time. And we have to know this, we have to know that; we have to prevent the trade from getting in. Suddenly, the feeling is that because it's electronic, we have to do more than we were doing in our normal operation. That isn't always the case.

Q. Since I've been watching the electronic end of the business, we've gone through three different types of technology, and each time it was the latest technology available. When I first came to LFG, they used a satellite system to provide equity runs, newsletters, and research. The second generation went into a dial-up, bulletin-board system. Dial-up technology was acceptable and got better, and just when it reached a high level of acceptance, we switched to the Internet version of the order entry system. For the past couple of years, since we've been on the Internet version, except for some upgrades, the basics have stayed the same. What, if anything, do you see as the next generation of technology in terms of what might be available, and how might it be applied to our situations here in the futures industry?

A. In the cases that you mentioned, it was the same business function being delivered by a different channel or method of delivery. We used just the satellite for delivery, which was one way of sending the stuff to people. Then we got into the bulletin boards or the dial-up modems, so now there were two ways they could ask a question or request what they wanted. Then, we went to the Internet. It was faster online, but still it was the same thing as the bulletin board, just a different delivery method. It was taking a different road to get to the same place. I think the next change, and we're already seeing it, is, again, the same. We are going to do the exact same thing, but only better.

Two advances that are going to be real big are wireless, so you are not tied to the physical line, and broadband. More wireless features are being integrated into cell phones. With the help of numeric pagers built into them, you can get e-mail with a wireless. With broadband, the amount of information that can be sent is increased. With a modem you are always limited to that modem speed. We started with LEO trading at 2400 baud; then we upgraded to the 9600-baud modems and then to the 56K modems. And then we had people on ISDN at 128K and now finally on broadband (cable or DSL). The same connections are now much faster, which allows us to send clients more than just what they needed to get the job done. Now you can have audio and video simultaneously so clients can actually see the research analyst showing them graphs and explaining his point of view or showing them the effect the weather is having on the crops. The broader band that we are able to transmit on now makes multiple functions more complete.

Q. So you're saying that in addition to the quicker, and possibly more reliable, order entry system, we are moving into an era where it will become like a personal TV, where you can get information on demand. Instead of turning on channel 11 at 8:00, you will be able to turn on your computer and request not only the information but also the person who wrote the report?

A. Exactly. Greenspan spoke at 2:00, and the commentary by the research analyst is out at 2:30. You could review that at 8:00 when you get home from work. You can see that actual conference and that video at the same time you view the graphs and the price feeds showing the impact of the report or the projections of it. You can watch your portfolio being priced simultaneously as you make a decision to buy or sell.

Q. So if you knew you wanted 10 research reports by 8:00, you could set it like you do your VCR and watch a half-hour customized news report on anything you want to know about, and nothing else?

A. Sure, since we have broadband to send a huge amount of information, and because we have the basic stable infrastructure in place, we can take advantage of more advanced features. Pinball machines are a classic example. It sounds odd, but pinball machines use 8008 microprocessor chips, a very old microchip. Yet it took a long time for manufacturers to take the technology to the field. Well, that time has also shrunk. It used to take 3 years from the time Intel came out with a chip before you saw a machine on the street. Now it only takes a few months. So now that we have all this delivery mechanism in place: the broadband, the wireless, the Internet, you can now build these other systems and features into it like the VCR timer aspect of pulling down reports. The technology is more intelligent, and that will continue to create new means of transmitting and selecting information.

Q. OK, help me put things in perspective in terms of how far we've come in a very short period of time. Comparing the modem-modem version, which seemed to be the slowest of all, comparing that to the most advanced technology we have today, are we comparing a Volkswagen to a Lear jet here in terms of speed, or are we comparing a Volkswagen to a Ferrari?

A. Probably in between. I'd say comparing the Volkswagen to an airplane, maybe not a Lear jet, but certainly air speed. I just had cable modem installed at my house. It's fantastic and incredibly fast. But at times you're still on the same street as everybody else, so there is still a lot of traffic that can slow you down. Or the server you are trying to talk to is still bogged down either because of traffic or because it's a slower, smaller machine, so you're waiting for them to be able to deliver the information. Once it's put on that pipe, it's fast getting to you, but you are still waiting for them to process the information or to be able to send it out.

Q. So your equipment and connection is only going to be as efficient as the equipment that you're hooking up to?

A. Right, that would be the limitation. It's only going to be as fast as the slowest link in the chain.

Q. In terms of technology, because other companies are all not exactly on a level playing field, is that a problem right now in the futures industry?

A. I wouldn't call it a problem. I'd say it's a transition that we are going through. My machine at home is a 200 Megahertz, and at the time I bought it, that was state of the art. It was fast, and it was fine when I was getting information downloaded at 28.8 or 36 bits, because by the time the graphics got to me, I was able to process it in time. Now that I have a cable modem, I realize I have a slow machine. Now I want a faster machine because I have a faster pipe. Regarding the public acceptance, we're over the hurdle now from both the company's and the customer's perspective. It's not a fad, and it's going to be around for a while. It is more than we ever expected.

You have children doing their homework and research over the Internet. And you have pipe fitters checking the Internet to look at vacation spots, so it's no longer just the academics or the traders who will proceed with this high tech. The Internet is just generally accepted now. You have a fax, you have an answering machine, and now, of course, you have the Internet. That acceptance, I think, has helped the whole of electronic trading. Before, the fear factor and lack of awareness that we were talking about when it was new was considered an impediment. I think you now see that mentality has got to the point that people trade only because they have an Internet connection and that they may never have thought of trading before. But now, because of the Internet and the increased knowledge and the access to the information, they feel they don't have to be an insider. Anybody can now go to Schwab and E-Trade. No one just puts money in his 401(k) anymore and lets it sit there while somebody else decides where to invest. Now with their 401(k) money, people are pointing and clicking with it everyday. I think that acceptance has helped a lot, maybe even more so at LFG than at other companies.

Interview with Charles Starnes

Charles Starnes is vice president of LFG, with responsibilities in Internet services, including order entry.

Q. What do you believe the company's needs are and what its potential needs will be in electronic trading? What do you think the customer is going to demand from the FCM in the future, knowing that maybe today the technology isn't there but tomorrow it will be there?

A. You've asked two questions, the first being about the FCM's needs and the second being about what the customer will demand from the FCM. Let me address the easier one first, the needs of the FCM and the cost of executing trades. The more a firm can do to automate order processing, the lower its cost will be on an incremental basis. So as we migrate toward complete automation, we will be more electronic than open outcry. As our cost goes down, we can pass that cost reduction on to our clients.

Q. As we go to a higher bandwidth, which will allow us to deliver more information, we will be able to have analysts read their reports so that clients can go to our web site at 8:00 at night and download just the research that was relevant to them. Do you believe FCMs, in addition to their clearing functions, will have to provide cutting-edge technology and in-depth timely research?

A. Absolutely. As much as I would like to think we could maintain an edge on electronic delivery from a standpoint of getting orders from the customer and getting fill information back to the customer—currently, we are at 2 to 3 seconds to get an order through Globex and back—I don't know if any further decrease in turnaround is going to help. Other firms will catch us in terms of their transmission speed capabilities. There are differences in the interfaces and other issues, such as browser-based programs having to wait for pages to load when they're switching from one screen to another, and those issues may be more important in the current environment. Even some of those issues have become less of a concern because of greater access to bandwidth, so whether it's browser-based or application-based probably won't make a significant difference in the future, If there is nothing else to differentiate their product, then FCMs will be driven to bring in business by driving down price, which cuts margins. Even if price is the issue, then the business we bring in may not be as secure as it once was when another firm is willing to match or undercut that price. Our customers will be looking for price and some other value we can add. So yes, I believe that it is imperative for FCMs who wish to succeed in this whole Internet society to offer something that customers find valuable in addition to basic order delivery and execution.

Q. There doesn't seem to be any move toward electronic standardization, which makes it more difficult for a company to develop products. What problems has the lack of standardization created for FCMs?

A. I don't really see a need for the standardization. We have managed to survive here for some time using the CBOT's and CME's TOPS interface, which also supports order flow for New York, Kansas City, Minneapolis, and so on. The reality is that there probably isn't that much value to the exchange in providing us with a standardized interface. In addition, there are competing end products. There are deck management tools in the hands of the brokers on the floor, for example. Some FCMs, including us, may want to be able to direct orders without having to go through the existing system. As long as the various exchanges provide an API, standardized interfaces for their platforms, then once you have a front end, to convert that front end to be able to interface with an API is really not that big of an issue. And it actually provides greater flexibility to route things in ways that we can't currently do. On a more specific basis, for example, we might have three different broker devices trading S&Ps and one group of customers may be routed to one device and another group of customers routed to a second device. Now everything has to go to the same device, so it's not as flexible.

Q. From a client perspective, the competition and the technology available within the industry seem to be at a high level in both areas right now. Do you think this will change?

A. I think the competition will continue to be there. From a technological standpoint, on a purely execution basis, differentiation is going to be difficult. To the extent that open outcry remains, executing trades there will provide some opportunity for differentiation based on specific brokers or broker groups that handle order flow. It may be that we will find it valuable and worthwhile to put our own broker in the pit and then to upgrade the level of that broker to the highest possible level in order to tout that capability and capacity. If we become more and more electronic, then this type of order flow will become less and less of an issue. What is going to be important is what tools we can give a customer to help that customer succeed.

Q. As liquidity increases in electronic trading, do you think there will be less and less of a need for the liquidity that the locals currently provide?

A. It's going to be interesting to see how we get from here to there. Comparing the securities industry with the futures industry right now, what you don't have in the futures industry are delegated market makers. For instance, at the CBOE, if I want to trade options, there will always be a market maker who is obligated to make a market, whether it's an electronic or an open-outcry environment. It really doesn't make that much of a difference, but there needs to be someone there to make a market. In the futures industry, its the local, the people on the floor that provide that liquidity in these corollary products that are quite important. You can see this with E-minis, for example. You can certainly put liquidity into an electronic marketplace as long as you're only trading the futures and only one contract month. Try to spread that out into multiple contract months in the same future and then add in all the various option contracts that go along with that, and we are nowhere close to having liquidity. The bid and offer size available in the option contracts just doesn't exist in Globex, for example. It only exists on the floor. So what the exchanges will do to change the way that they do business or what customers will do to change the way they perceive the business will be critical. To effect a change from open outcry to electronics we will need to address those issues. Without that we will eventually lose the liquidity in the electronic market.

Q. If you were in an office pool to pick the date that the exchange floor would close, what would your guess be?

A. I would say it's years, about 3 to 4 years. It could be extended or shortened depending on how the exchanges and the marketplace address some of the issues. I don't have a clear picture yet of a solution that will work. The difficulty in going to an all-electronic market is a little more problematic than I think many people realize.

Q. At times electronic trading lacks the liquidity necessary to provide proper fills for clients. Should there be circuit breakers when we hit a lack of liquidity?

A. I don't know if I agree with the idea of circuit breakers. We already have circuit breakers on the downside. Nobody expected we would need circuit breakers on the upside, so they're not in place. Certainly circuit breakers are not a bad idea if executed properly, and might be worth doing in that kind of marketplace. Sometimes electronics are so fast—in fact, too quick—that individuals can't react fast enough. They look for opportunities to take profits; they look for the opportunity to "arb" different markets into line when one market gets out of line versus another, cash versus futures, and so on and so forth. But no matter how fast they are, making decisions that quickly in front of a runaway market is hard. Electronics makes the reaction time required that much quicker. There are a couple of things that could happen that would make this less of a problem. Some of them are scary and some of them less scary. For instance, take an automated, hands-off trading system that reacts quickly to situations. The others are more mechanical systems that would allow for circuit breaker systems to go into effect to ensure liquidity.

Interview with Patrick Catania

Patrick Catania is the CBOT executive vice president for business development. In addition to this post, Catania is adjunct professor of finance, Western Illinois University, and is staff editor of *The Review of Futures Markets*, which is published by the Chicago Board of Trade. The review covers futures options and their underlying cash markets, including both empirical and theoretical work.

Q. I've noticed a shift in the Board of Trade's position. I don't know whether that is an institutional shift or just a shift that is motivated by the business and by the times. I am curious about your thoughts, about what you foresee happening in the future and when the future is most likely to take place.

A. To answer, let me briefly touch on some history. In 1980 I was director of business development for the first electronic exchange, Intex, out of Bermuda. At that time, if you got together with a venture capitalist and had the idea to trade futures electronically, the business went offshore because it was felt that the regulatory environment would be more palatable to everyone; and, in fact, its listings at that time were cleared through the LCCH (London Commodity Clearing House) for financial integrity. So all the pieces were there, and what people were doing was trying to respond to the same thing I'm seeing today—the exact same circumstances. The firms at that time, the large Wall Street firms, had huge costs to trade futures in open outcry. The exchange fees were negligible. It was the cost of the people managing the books, the phone clerks, the back-office staff, the margin clerks, etc., that created a very poor performance compared with the return on equity they were getting in other areas of the firm. Nothing has changed. I've heard this for 20 years, the same complaint, and that's why you see a number of firms try to get their own start-ups going, cash markets trading like either Liberty or

BrokerTec. Now BrokerTec's filing for contract market designation with the CFTC. When you look at the objective of every one of these entities over 20 years, it's the same thing: dealing with cost. Internally as we moved through electronic trading here at the Board of Trade, the eye was toward certainly remaining competitive by having electronic components, because we thought there was a whole market segment that just wanted to trade electronically. It was more convenient for a fund manager or other large customer to have a terminal on his desk and be able to execute directly through a clearing member the types of trades he wanted to do.

As part of my duties here, I continually book meetings with our member firms, with our customers, and get our president and our chairman before these customers to hear their concerns. They feel torn. They love the parts of open outcry where they get the a sense of what's going on. They can talk to a person who sees where the orders are coming from and basically can tell exactly what the market is and what size it could absorb. At the same time they're still getting hammered by the firm's management committee in that they're returning 12 percent on capital and other divisions are returning 25 percent or 30 percent.

Some months ago the Board of Trade decided that we had to get further into electronic trading. We had to bring technology to our open-outcry markets if they were going to exist at all—technology in the form of getting orders in and out, getting them to the clearinghouse, taking them out of the hands that touch the paper, getting the paper out of the process. We were told by many firms that if we were to take that step, their costs would be reduced significantly and that open-outcry and electronic trading could exist in some sort of a side-by-side mode. The problem that we face in undertaking that strategy, and by the way, that is our current strategy, is to build this harmonious integrated open-outcry–electronic trading system.

Q. So what you have is a common back-office platform in terms of reducing the number of people and paper?

A. Exactly. A common back-office platform with an open API that allows the firms to do whatever they want to do on the front end that is compatible once it hooks to our pipe. We believe that this model would be most powerful. It's kind of like trying to satisfy everyone and everyone's need. The problem is, and it's no secret, it's real expensive for the exchange in the initial phases to put all these things into place. We have the expense of the routing system and the attached back-office systems to monitor. At the same time, we've chosen to go with Eurex as our alliance partner to put together an electronic trading platform, and we have huge costs in software development in building that system. Those costs, by the way, while they're high, are about what we had estimated it would have cost us to take our existing Project A and make that blossom into the same type of system that could serve a global market. So we're facing similar costs.

I think the surprise is what it's costing us to make open outcry change to integrate into this system. We're taking steps to go so far as to allow our floor traders to have a handheld unit that they can integrate with and that lets them hit and take what they see on the screen. Our objective is to bring the liquidity on the floor onto the screen, and the customer orders that we anticipate being largely screen-directed give the people on the floor a chance to trade against those customer orders and have some semblance of what they have today, an opportunity to trade against the orders whether they are directed to open outcry or whether they come into the electronic venue. Again, the estimates of what it costs to run the exchanges are just surprising. They continue to keep us very conscious of the day-to-day dollar expenditures around the entire exchange. Not that we shouldn't do that all the time anyway, but this has been critical, and I guess the overriding concern for us now is that when we built our new trading floor in 1997, we elected to pay that debt down in very short order. We didn't take that 20-year mortgage or what you might suspect, and so the debt payment schedule we have on that building is impacting our ability to roll out these technology answers in a timely fashion. So that's where we're at today.

Q. When you compare Eurex and some of the other European platforms with the U.S. markets, do you see the same forces at work here that were in Europe, or is the nature of the customer and the business itself different enough to sustain open outcry for a period of time?

A. I'm leaning toward the path that says "We're different enough to sustain open outcry for a period of time," and that perspective is largely due to the fact that if you compare us with other exchanges either that were always electronic or that converted, such as LIFFE, from open outcry to electronic, they did not have the large customer base on the floor that we have. Our internal trade, our member-driven trade, is about 52 percent of our volume in some of the key contracts. So when you stop and think, if you go back to LIFFE in the early days, there were floor traders and what they call locals, but they were not guys that took thousand lots and redistributed them 10 times out the pit. These were guys that basically tried to race the orders when they saw big buys or big sells coming in, and I don't think they ever achieved the customer base on their floor that we have here. In a marketing position, I've been conscious of this for years, because when you segment your markets and you look at your customers, then you attempt to target your activity. I've always got a large piece of my effort directed to an internal customer base that provides 50 percent of the business in a number of our contracts.

Q. In regard to the Board of Trade's timing, do you see any advantage for the Board of Trade in terms of being able to be technically smart at this moment in time and to take advantage of those advances that have been built up over the last 3 or 4 years?

A. The question is, would you rather be lucky or smart? We may be lucky in that regard, because I'm sure you know the structure here of a membership organization and it has caused us to move slowly. I think in some ways that has been beneficial. I think at the end of the day anyone in this business still faces the same kind of costs involved in making a conversion or in building a system initially. That really remains our biggest hurdle, the cost to pull this off. I think it's fair to say we're operating two exchanges and we're doing it with a diminished staff and I think the staff will be even more diminished as we go forward. There's so much uncertainty about whether or not we'll be all electronic, or whether or not we'll maintain two exchanges, and many people are making career decisions at a time when employment is good and opportunities are plentiful. So we're faced with an additional variable in the equation here of being able to man this whole transition.

The Board has been working on a restructuring plan, and that plan is coming to fruition. We expect to get a membership vote in the near future to take the company to a for-profit status and to change the governance to the degree that we can act quickly and react quickly to market conditions. All of this may be just coming together at the right time, and having been slow to act early on may be a benefit for us. I'm confident of that, particularly if we're able to keep our volume levels where they are, which are a little bit lower than a year ago but pretty close. By the way as a side note, our bellwether contract has plummeted in volume. The long bond is off substantially, some 40 percent. Cash market trading in the long bond is off 70 percent, but at the same time our 10-year note and 5-year note have picked up 67 percent and 53 percent, respectively. They started from smaller bases so we haven't made up all that bond value yet. I'm confident if we keep our overall volumes at current levels, financially we'll be able to fund these two entities until we can kick into gear and see if the theory is in fact going to pull through.

Q. As you look at this demutualization process that is going through all the exchanges, do you get a sense that if the demutualization is accomplished, there would be a better atmosphere for cooperation among the exchanges in terms of the domestic linkage of futures exchanges in New York and the two exchanges in Chicago?

A. I believe very strongly that that's a possibility. Very simplistically, you end up dealing with a management committee and a small board, and you are not dealing with member petitions and member votes. If you put a handful of businesspeople in a room and they determine there's a business purpose to make an arrangement, or make a merger, or cooperate, then it can be done. We've missed many opportunities over the years, as have most of the exchanges. Business groups from the outside had ways to augment our business or tie into our business. Now with the E-Commerce Group there's geometric exposure to a number of those opportunities, and I think the exchanges are all positioning themselves to better take advantage of them. They could include mergers or linkages among those exchanges or between any two of them. There are a lot more possibilities, and I think the economies of scale and just pure business sense will drive that.

As you know, we're talking with the CBOE right now; and we started the CBOE in 1973, and regulatory reasons forced us to divest of that exchange. Many people have felt the derivatives, in options, equity options, and futures and options, should all be bundled into one shop anyway, so there's an initial example if we get something done with those folks or even if it's delayed until after restructuring and we then move ahead. That's an example of the opportunity of a consolidated exchange.

Q. When you look at the European exchanges and the U.S. exchanges in terms of the customer base, what consideration has the CBOT given to ease of use for the retail end user, rather than an institutional base looking at a large retail customer base?

A. I think the consideration that the CBOT is giving has been to modify our access rules in terms of a membership institution. We have relaxed the restrictions to get access to the terminals under the Eurex platform alliance. Formerly you had to buy a full membership, and only in your business location could you have a Project A terminal or an electronic trading system. Under the new rules, these terminals can be placed anywhere and you need only have a leased associate membership, which dropped down to around a hundred thousand dollars. So the cost of entry has been greatly reduced, and the restriction on where terminals can go has been reduced. There's recognition of the importance of those customers, and we realize the access policy of Eurex really counts for their growth. Its terminals are in every money manager's shop, in every pension fund manager's office, and at every bank trading desk, so distribution of terminals and open access are key to the potential for success.

Q. When you look at BrokerTec, an institutionally based entity that has applied for trade status or contract market status, what is the likelihood, and this is pure speculation, that there will be tension between the larger members of the CBOT and the institution itself where these members take the attitude that perhaps we don't need the CBOT any longer? Perhaps they can create their own contracts and can do their own clearing.

A. I wouldn't call it tension, because I think that feeling has existed for years, and there have been other attempts by firms to try and break off and clear. In fact, the Bermuda Electronic Exchange I referenced was headed by Merrill Lynch. A gentleman named Gene Grumner was their global futures director and was asked about that issue, that attempt, and that was 20 years ago. There are certainly two sides to this argument. There are the firms and the exchange, and you would think that the firms were trying to pull away and do everything themselves, but what complicates matters is that within the firms there's not agreement. The guy sitting at the capital markets desk who knows he's got to sell a thousand 10-year notes is not going to put them through the firm's trading system until it can provide him exactly the same liquidity as or better liquidity than he's able to get here. So they have their own dissension within the firms, and we can go visit the same firm in three different locations in the same building and get at least two different opinions on this whole thing. I think within the firms the guys who read the P&Ls and see the returns, and see that the futures division isn't earning what it should be earning, they see a lot clearer picture of how much profit they could make if they ran it themselves. On the other side of the coin, the guys that generate the real volumes for them are guys that could pick up and take their book and walk out of that firm's office and go down the street and bring that business to where they can trade the way they want to trade. That's really the aspect that's driven us to try to keep open outcry as competitive as possible, because continually we get input from those kinds of guys. When push comes to shove, that's how they want to trade. Many of these guys don't even want a terminal on their desk. They don't want the risk of execution; they don't want the error risk; they want to just pick up a phone, give the order, and get done and go onto the next trade. It's clearly the whole market segment, and you've got to look at these different segments. I guess the trick is to determine where the most value potential is and where you put your most effort in terms of building a system or marketplace that will satisfy that heavy level in volume.

Q. From a regulatory perspective in terms of the influence of the CFTC and the lesser influence of the NFA, do

you have a perspective on the effect of electronic trading, particularly on the efforts of the federal regulators and how the move toward electronic trading will either lessen their authority or increase their authority?

A. I don't know whether it lessens or increases their authority, but I think clearly they, the regulators, believe that electronic trading increases their ability to regulate. They are infatuated with the AuditTrack concept, where they can see who trades what with whom, when, how many, where, and how. They've been a little slow to address the issues of prearranged trading where in thinner markets two guys are on the telephone for 5 minutes first and then miraculously a thousand trades go off at a given price. But I do think that they believe that electronic trading makes what they see as their job a lot easier. And they've embraced it. There's no secret about it. They've approved all kinds of electronic systems. Whether it's E-Speed and the Cantor Exchange, or whether its Eurex doing business in the states or overseas, they're totally sold on that concept as regulators. The systems that we've had in open outcry here for monitoring the computerized trade reconstruction and those types of systems have gotten to the level where they were 94 or 95 percent accurate and the regulators were satisfied. I think they believe they've gone one step further in electronic trading, so they're going to back it to any extent that they can. I haven't seen any efforts by regulators to say let's do monitoring with open-outcry trading, but I do know that they feel more comfortable in electronic trading in terms of the ability to audit it.

Q. Does the CBOT have a sense that the ideal on electronic trading has broadened its customer base from a retail account perspective?

A. It believes that it can't but help. In fact we would expect our Dow contract alone to double or triple in volume when the customers can come right through their personal computers at home into the firm's pipe and go right to an electronic execution—much the same as the E-mini has at the Mercantile Exchange. That's demonstrated the potential for that retail trade, and there is no question that we want to capture that trade in this system that we're developing and that we will in fact be able to do that.

Q. With the CBOT then, given that perspective and looking at what the Merc has done with various E-mini contracts, will the CBOT want to create its own smaller-sized contracts to make them more accessible to the public?

A. We've looked at that for a long time and especially in the area of the grain contracts, because that's where a lot of retail interest gets focused. When a new account opens, nine out of ten guys put the account into a corn contract because it does move but it's not going to blow their heads off if they're wrong. The fact of the matter is, if you look at those contracts, they're "minis" already. You see, 5000 bushel contracts in corn is about $11,000. If you look at soybeans, 5000 bushels is a $25,000 contract. Now consider the old S&P. It was in the neighborhood of $600,000, and our bond contracts were at $100,000. You can see that all our retail-type contracts are really in that neck of the woods; they're affordable. The fact of the matter is, if we promoted them that way, we'd have much greater business, but there's no sense to promote them in that fashion until we have the systems capability to handle that business. So that's why you've seen little in that area until our Eurex platform is built.

Q. What is the overall sense of the membership at the CBOT in terms of ongoing business of the CBOT in this electronic environment? Is it positive, or is it negative?

A. I really don't know what the mood of the 3500 is. I know personally from members I deal with all the time, either in a committee structure or just personal friends, that there has been a dramatic shift in the last couple of years, so much as even a willingness to learn systems and how to work them. My division is responsible for training for all the electronic systems, and we've had a dramatic increase in the number of guys who just signed up for Project A classes, even without intending to take the screen but wanting to have the knowledge of how to use it. From that perspective, I can tell you there's been a definite shift in attitude. About the only measurement stick that I have is that kind of a response to what we're doing in the training arena. We even have a general session on compatibility and computer literacy. We've offered the membership a number of classes in that route. It's very similar to what we went through about 8 or 9 years ago when we introduced agricultural options. My classes were filled with new young guys who wanted to trade options. But I never saw the full members who were trading corn and soybeans and who had everything to gain by learning how to trade options so they could have another tool to mitigate their own risk and enhance their trading returns. We ran special classes where you had to be a full member to even get into the class, and it took several years before they availed themselves of those classes. And now, today, you look around and you'll see a lot of full members trading the agricultural options on a regular basis and still maintaining their trading positions in the corn pit or the bean pit or whatever. It's a learning curve. For some people it's real steep, and for other people it's more graduated. They're all on it at some point.

Q. In the best of all possible worlds as we look at the matters we've touched on, in terms of cost, in terms of regulatory issues, and in terms of member support, exchange support, and the ability to develop the technology, if you could look into your crystal ball, how far out do you see a fully integrated viable electronic exchange coming out of the CBOT?

A. I think we take the first big step this fall or late this summer with the Eurex platform. I think that the second phase, which doesn't integrate many Eurex members in our product line, will be the step that crosses that bridge. So I can see integration coming within the next 12 months. In terms of enhancements to the open-outcry market that will further bring that transition into play, I think those are being done simultaneously with the rollout in the systems. Certainly you are going to have a decision point, whether or not the theory was correct that open outcry and electronic can coexist, and you'll be in position either way if in fact it is coexisting and you're seeing volume growth in both venues, as opposed to just the electronic venue siphoning off on a gradual basis. If you do see that growth in both venues, you'll know you're right and move farther down that path. If you see the siphoning activity, but at a slower rate than we saw at other places, you may even choose to accelerate that transition so as not to have double costs for operations over a longer period of time. I think that decision point is somewhere in the next 12 months.

Interview with Donald Serpico

Donald Serpico is executive vice president of operations for the Chicago Mercantile Exchange, responsible for all trading floor operations, trading floor support, and telecommunications including the direct interface with the MIS systems; all the systems that are used on the trading floor; all the telephones at the CME; and all other communication lines, such as the CUBS application, TOPS application. handheld, price reporting, and all Globex systems on the trading floor. He is also responsible for the direct relationship and interface with the MIS staff who maintain that equipment and provide support for the equipment on the trading floor.

From the standpoint of operational procedures, his responsibilities include fixing systems and monitoring the performance of those systems, as well as monitoring any construction changes or operational changes on the trading floor and the telephones in the towers and on the trading floors.

Q. Let's go back to when Globex1 first began. You were responsible for getting involved in setting up the infrastructure of that, right?

A. Yes, the division for that started all the way back toward the end of 1986, and then in 1987 we started to give life to it by looking at the idea of working with a provider, a market data service provider, so we could utilize that provider's network to facilitate electronic trading primarily in the evening. The whole idea was given birth by the number of EFPs, or exchange for physicals, that were being executed at night and the opportunity we wanted to gain by providing other markets in other time zones, by using our products in our own facility. And to that end, we looked at a number of different vendors. We chose Reuters as the company we wanted to deal with, and we entered into a contract. We worked on the system primarily in the later part of the eighties and early part of the nineties and implemented it in 1992.

Q. When you began working on Globex, you didn't have off-the-shelf programs like we do today. What were some of the problems that you faced because technology was not as advanced as it is now?

A. First of all, if you're looking at an electronic trading system, it's a little different from what you need on the trading floor. On the trading floor back then, using handheld and portable devices was very difficult, because hardware technology wasn't sufficient. For instance, from the standpoint of what you needed as far as battery life, the weight of the unit, the size of the unit, and the whole organic infrastructure, not to mention the application that you would have to build around that, the trading applications or the EP routing applications or what have you were not readily available. But in the electronic trading system what we primarily needed was the ability to have a robust enough engine that would do the matching, the logic behind the program, and a network and terminals you trade on. Even back then in the eighties there were terminals you could trade on. These were being used in other marketplaces for cash market trading. There was nobody doing futures trading back at that time, so we were really leading the pack on this.

What we needed to do was to find somebody who had a network, somebody who had an application that we could modify and a front-end structure, or the terminal imputing side, that would take the applications, if you will, that would allow people to use the terminal to put the bids and the offers in and the buys and the sells in, and manage the trades, the orders, and the partial lots and other things you need in the electronic trading system. Back then the closest thing we could find was Reuters. They had a system for cash market trading that we used as a building block to build a futures system. So to say that it was not as advanced as it is today is absolutely right. There were no OM systems; there were no other exchange systems that we could draw on. We literally had to go to Reuters and have them modify their system for a futures environment. So that's where the task was in building the application. As far as people having the terminal support, the networks, and even trading engines to do cash market–type trades or those types of instruments that you would find in the security industry, we knew that we could draw on those, but what we had to do was write the application that would work for the futures market, and that was the big task.

Q. I've noticed at least two instances in the past where there has been a lack of liquidity, either above or below the market, and the E-mini contract seemed to overreact to that situation. What do you foresee that might act to correct that within the computer?

A. Actually we have some fail-safes in place now that, if managed correctly by the member firms and their customers, could be very effective. I'll give you a couple of examples. If you are dealing with customers who are trading on a terminal for their own accounts, we have what we call the basic credit controls for a firm. No one can trade Globex at the present time without going through a member firm, a clearing firm. We will not allow end users to come directly to us. They have to go through a clearing firm. In that regard, there are basic checks and balances that ask what limits do you want on a customer. You can limit by contract size and by the price movement. You limit the number of positions a client can put on—something as simple as a customer putting the wrong entry in. The computer will ask the question, do you really want to do this? And then the customer has to overwrite it for approval. That's basically what we call a dummy alert, which is basically saying do you really want to do something like this; and if the customer does override, it will take it.

The firm's second check on customers consists of the true credit controls where the system will not let customers place an order. Those facilities are in these systems. Firms can embellish these by putting into place their own safeguard systems that can interface with Globex. Beyond these we do literally have circuit breakers. We follow the same rules in the E-mini that we follow for the S&P 500. Whenever we get a circuit breaker in the 500, it causes an immediate halt in the E-mini. This has been in place ever since we started the E-mini. You may see situations in the E-mini where the market sort of runs away with you. I'll give you an example. I will not mention the firm, but there were situations where the firm did not have the correct controls. A client would go off the market, creating an advantage, and someone would pick that client off. It was obvious the person made a mistake. That's where you can see, depending upon the exchange and how it administers these kinds of situations, you have fair trade policies. Here you get the buyer and seller together, and they present their case to a committee administered by the Globex Control Center. Most of the exchanges doing this have these fair trade policies, and they make a decision based upon how far the customer was off the market. Typically what will happen is one firm will write another firm a check to make up for the difference, but they will resolve the major differences. In some cases, they will split it in half; in other cases, if it's way off the market and the advantaged party accepts that it was truly a mistake, the exchange will allow the GCC to bust the trade.

Q. So what you're saying is, as we begin to see new problems that we did not anticipate, the exchange will usually take action that will be fair to both the client and the member firms.

A. Absolutely, within reason. That's where fair trade policy comes into play, but even before you get to that, we have the circuit breakers and the firm has credit controls and dummy alerts, so you have all those facilities, and some of those are automated. Of course, the fair trade policy is not automated, but members of a committee are actually available and on call in the event that we run into a fair trade issue, and the GCC does administer that very well.

Q. What new products do you see coming out within the next couple of years that we don't have today?

A. We have some on the horizon. In the next couple of months we will have a weather product that we are very excited about. It's one that will measure temperature, in eight different cities. We are starting off with four cities, and then we're going to add four cities one month later. That's going to be totally on Globex, electronic only, and that will allow us to work off an index of a certain temperature, the midpoint of which is 65 degrees. It will be used as a good hedge mechanism for people whose business relies on the weather. We're moving in an environment where we'll probably have more E-minis. So I would say that in the future you will see more products based upon a mini version of the major product.

Q. What do you believe is the biggest challenge that futures exchanges face right now from a technological perspective?

A. A couple of things. First of all you have seen all these alliances. The Board of Trade has completed an alliance with the German Exchange, or Eurex. We just announced last week that we have formed an alliance with LIFFE (London International Financial Futures Exchange) and the New York Mercantile Exchange has formed an exchange with IPE (International Petroleum Exchange) in London. I think the major challenge, however, is really with the systems in place right now. We have to make these systems transparent to the end users so that they don't have to buy a lot of hardware. In that regard, we all have to find ways to connect Globex Project A or LIFFE together in order to allow the end users to work on a terminal without having to know how all the systems fit together at the back end. We have to allow them to have a transparent way to get in each of those markets from the same terminal; that's a challenge. In this regard we are working with LIFFE to make that connection.

The second challenge we have is within our own systems. Within Globex proper, the trading engine, you have to have a very robust system, one that gives you performance, reliability, and functionality. A lot of us are now sharpening our competitive edges. The advantage is drawn with a far finer line than we've ever seen. To keep the advantage you have to get into more product features than you've ever had before, and they have to be more sophisticated. If you look at our Eurodollar product as an example, our side-by-side Eurodollar product is, from a technology functionality standpoint, a very complex product because of all the packs and bundles and spreads and all the different ways you can trade those 40 contracts months. To do that electronically is a challenge. But we have to meet that challenge, because if we don't, somebody else will take that product away from us. In the second area, from a competitive standpoint, you have to keep your technology up to date. Your performance has to be there, and you have to be reliable. That's the second challenge. So connectivity to other exchange systems and keeping your own systems functionally rich and technically rich are new challenges.

Interview with John Rand

John Rand is an independent trader at the Chicago Mercantile Exchange. He began his trading career at the Chicago Board of Trade in the late 1970s and then went to the Chicago Board Options Exchange in the early 1980s. He worked for Oppenheimer for 5 years as a manager and floor broker on the CBOE. From 1985 to 1988 he was at Drexel Burnham, where, as the operational manager in the S&P 100 index (OEX), he executed orders for institutional customers and retail customers. In the 1990s he started trading on his own in the OEX. In 1994 he came to the Merc for the first time with Timber Hill, starting up a NASDAQ project. In 1997, he worked with the Chicago Futures Group on the Exploratory Committee setting up the E-mini project. He was a broker there for approximately a year and had the distinction of being the first broker to trade the E-mini contract. He recently set up an account with ZAP Futures, trading electronically off the floor.

Q. You've had a lot of experience in the business, mostly nonelectronic because when you started there were no electronics. Let's start with Timber Hill. Timber Hill was one of the first companies to introduce electronics in many different forms for its client base. Could you give me a little background on that?

A. Timber Hill is an operation out of New York where it would hedge equity premium versus index premium, and it would play the market for the institutional customers, and now it is introducing retail customer business. Timber Hill has wireless handheld computers on the trading floor, and it will make a market in any option or any equity on the floor.

Q. So the ability was there to deliver the trades via electronics at that time, which was in what, 1994?

A. It was not primitive but close to it. We had a lot of electrical problems, a lot of communication problems as to where the system would go down, and it was on the verge of blossoming. As of today they're much better at it, that's for sure.

Q. You were trading in a pit as an open-outcry broker, and you were also trading in a pit as an electronic broker. As a matter of fact, you were one of the first brokers to trade the E-mini contract, right?

A. I was the first broker in the E-mini pit. I was with Chicago Futures Group at that time. I was a broker representing customer orders for the firm. I also represented market makers in the S&P options pit as well as the futures pit where they would hedge futures positions with E-mini positions. Fortunately enough, the exchange allowed me to fill customer paper and trade for my own account.

Q. With being the first broker in the E-mini pit, not only was the technology new, but also the experience of trading in a different way was new. What were some of the advantages and some of the disadvantages that you saw?

A. The E-mini started up in September of 1998; the previous December is when the exchange cut the contract in half. The handle on a contract was $500 at the time they cut it in half, and then they did the exploratory about getting the E-mini started. This is just my own opinion, but if they would have kept the contract as is, at $500 per handle, and introduced the E-mini, I think it would have been more successful than it actually is today. Obviously it's becoming successful, more successful, but I think the E-mini would have had a pit to itself. But the funny thing about the E-mini is that it allowed smaller traders with less capitalization to actively trade the markets. It allowed a lot of people to come in and trade the smaller lots versus the big contract or accumulate positions against the big contracts, which are always hedged. I really think it was a great concept. The potential is huge; right now as you can see, the volume is exceeding 70,000 contracts a day.

Q. One of the advantages of being a broker in the E-mini pit is that it overlooks the S&P pit, and there are opportunities for arbitrage. At the beginning of the concept of the contract there was not as much liquidity. They were trading 5000 a day as opposed to 50,000 a day. Did you find it

more difficult or was it easier during the time when the E-minis and the big contract didn't track each other as closely? Was it better for you being able to arbitrage it, or did the opportunities come and go too quickly?

A.   To be honest with you, at the very beginning there were some disparities where you could buy the E-mini at even while the big contract was 10 cents bid or 20 cents bid. You could make a quick couple of ticks on it. The disparity wasn't really there that much; I mean there were opportunities. My background was technical and fundamental, so if I had a feel for the market, I would always lead the way with minis, and accumulate toward the big contract, where I would by two or three minis and let the big contract lead the way and then accumulate some more and then offset it on the big contract or in the minis. The big advantage at that time was the open-outcry system. At the time, 30 or more contracts had to be done open outcry. Those were the opportunities, because if a customer would come in, I could not trade against my customer's orders. I could participate with my customers on the same side, but I couldn't take the position from them. There was another executing broker, and the opportunities that presented themselves were moneymaking times. At that time the whole thing was not sophisticated enough, I still needed a crowd clerk who would watch me, I still needed an executing broker in the S&P futures pit that basically knew my trading style. Let's suppose I bought a 30 lot of E-minis, I would have to do six big contracts against that. Now if my clerk wasn't watching me at that time and my broker didn't know what I was trying to do, it would probably be a losing trade and not a moneymaking trade. The mechanics were there. Globex1 worked very well. But Globex2 was introduced a little too early in my estimation, and that's one of the reasons why I left. It wasn't as user friendly as Globex1 was.

Q. You're currently trading through the ZAP high-speed, online futures order entry system from your house. You probably don't have the exact same scalping opportunities from your house because you're not sitting in the pit, so you're not able to arbitrage the way you were doing. Do you find this easier or harder now that you're trading out of your house for yourself, rather than standing in the pit trading for yourself? How would you compare the two?

A. At this point I find it much easier and less stressful simply because I can look at a chart pattern. And as I said before, my background has been technical, so I can see patterns develop, formulate an opinion, put in my buy stop or sell stop, get involved in the market, place my stop orders for limited risk, and watch the market move, hopefully, in my direction.

Q. Do you find yourself following your system more when you're away from the emotional atmosphere of the pit?

A. I don't necessarily have a system. It's more of a methodology watching the market's overbought-oversold conditions, knowing from my experience in the psychology of the crowd where the market is pushed by the locals back and forth. Those are the times where the extremes are stretched out to the max, and those are the times to get in, instead of being pushed around by the crowd. Fortunately enough, I think using electronic trading I could be anywhere, have an opinion, and place my orders. The nice thing about electronic trading with the ZAP system is that I can still call into the ZAP

Desk and place my orders. And if I'm hooked up to the Internet, I can trade anywhere in the world.

Q. You mention the psychology of the crowd; a lot of this book is based on taking a look at the psychology of trading as well as some of the technical issues. Often, being in the pit makes you think of being in a very large gambling palace where people are playing craps, because both are very high energy types of situations, and emotions tend to fly very high. One of the biggest downfalls of any trader, whether in the pit or outside the pit, is letting emotions get in your way. The fact that you're able to take a step back and be a little more relaxed, is that making you feel any different?

A. Absolutely, because the emotions are taken away. Obviously you still have emotions when the market goes against you, but when you do not have the crowd reaction, especially on something like a news item, you have a better feel. It's like you're wearing blinders. My own personal reason why I left the trading floor is that I'm not getting any younger, and I think it has a lot to do with the pressure of yelling and screaming all day long. It's a physical task. You don't get spit on anymore, and you don't have to be abused—this is definitely the way to go.

Q. Do you think that the playing field is becoming more level between the individual investor and the professional investor because of the high-speed electronics that are available, as well as the wealth of information that is now available over the Internet?

A. In certain aspects the playing field is more level. You have to understand the philosophy of the local traders. They are there to make small purchases—small sales for the fast buck. I think you have that opportunity trading off the floor now. I could look and scalp the markets, and I still have that ability. I think a lot of people without that experience cannot do that because they get caught up in the trade. For their advantage they are able to get into a trade and stay in it for a longer period. My experience when I was on the trading floor was never to be in a trade more than 5 to 10 minutes, and being off the floor now it feels like a lifetime, but in actuality it's nothing.

Q. You mentioned 5 to 10 minutes on the floor as a quick scalp trade. Has that time remained constant or changed any?

A. Actually, that's even a long time on the trading floor. If you want instant gratification, if you buy something at even and someone's trying to buy it at 10 or 20, you're going to sell it to them. Being off the trading floor you tend to stretch out your trades because there are levels when to be long and when to be short. In this marketplace that's the most important thing, because you don't want to get caught up. You can be on a trade, and if it goes against you, you may get stopped out and those are the hardest trades to reenter.

Q. With your new style of trading, are you risking the same as the market goes above or below a certain risk point? Are you going to get out no matter what the system, whether it's in your house or on the floor? Are you saying that because you're in your house and removed from the floor, if a trend does develop in the right direction for you, you might have a tendency to hold onto that trade much longer?

A. Correct. That's the ultimate goal.

Q. I guess that's the name of the game—cut your losses quickly and let your profits rise. So this move is forcing you to trade a little differently and possibly a little better.

A. Absolutely right. I hopefully am going to be working smarter in my life and not harder. That's the key to trading.

Interview with Leo Melamed

Leo Melamed, chairman emeritus and senior policy advisor of the Chicago Mercantile Exchange, is recognized as the founder of financial futures. As chairman of the CME, Melamed in 1972 launched the International Monetary Market (IMM)—the first futures market for financial instruments. In the following years, Melamed led the CME in the introduction of a diverse number of financial instruments, including gold, Treasury bills, Eurodollars, and in 1982, stock index futures. Melamed has been a primary force in the U.S. futures industry, helping establish its markets as indispensable tools in financial risk management. In 1987, Melamed spearheaded the introduction of Globex, the world's first electronic futures trading system. In 1999, *Chicago Magazine,* as well as the editor of the *Chicago Tribune,* named Leo Melamed among the 100 most important Chicagoans of the twentieth century.

Melamed has been an advisor to the Commodity Futures Trading Commission and serves as special advisor on futures markets to governments worldwide. In 1982, Melamed led the futures industry effort before the U.S. Congress in creating the National Futures Association (NFA), a self-regulatory body of the futures industry. He served as chairman of the NFA from its inception until 1989 and continues to serve as its permanent special advisor. Melamed has lectured and written extensively on the subject of financial futures and free markets. He was editor of *An Anthology: The Merits of Flexible Exchange Rates,* published by George Mason University Press in 1988. He authored *Leo Melamed on the Markets,* a historical overview of the evolution of futures markets, published by John Wiley & Sons in 1993. In 1984, Melamed wrote a science fiction novel, *The Tenth Planet,* published by Bonus Books. *Escape to the Futures,* Melamed's memoirs, was published by John Wiley & Sons in 1996.

Leo Melamed is the recipient of numerous awards and special appointments: In 1979, the University of Chicago Graduate School of Business (GSB) established the Leo Melamed Prize for "a work of outstanding scholarship by a business school professor." Additionally, in 1991, the University of Chicago GSB established the Leo Melamed endowed chair for the study of futures markets. In 1992, President George Bush appointed Melamed to the Council of the United States Holocaust Memorial Museum, where he serves as a member of its executive committee. In 1998, the Weizmann Institute of Science established the Betty and Leo Melamed scholarship in biomedical research. In 1999, Melamed received an honorary degree of doctor of letters from the University of Illinois. Melamed serves on the board of directors of the National Bureau of Economic Research and is a senior fellow of the International Association of Financial Engineers.

Melamed is an attorney by profession and an active futures trader. He is chairman and CEO of Sakura Dellsher, Inc., a global futures organization formed in 1993 between the Sakura Bank, Ltd., and Dellsher Investment Company, Inc.

Q. How did electronic trading get started?

A. The beginnings of electronic trading came in connection to the mutual offset with the SIMEX; origination is important because one led to the other. The first step was the SIMEX, but in my mind, even though mutual offset was extremely successful, I didn't think we could duplicate that very easily everywhere in the world. We had to find an easier mechanism to protect ourselves from competition on a time zone–to–time zone basis. That was one of the thought processes that led to the Globex idea. The other one was simply my understanding that the computer could do these types of transactions.

Q. Right now with electronic trading there are strong proponents and there is strong resistance. Does this compare with the introduction of prior innovations?

A. In a small way maybe, but not as similar as you think. It's similar in the respect that anything that is a departure from the status quo is difficult to accept by the establishment. So by virtue of that comparison, between trading in currencies versus the agriculture world, there was a major leap in innovation. In a similar fashion perhaps, that leads to electronic trading also being a major innovation, and the resistance by establishment as well. That comparison does not go far enough, nor is it really fair to the two events. The introduction of foreign currency futures, which I pioneered in 1972, was a huge departure from maybe 5000 years of history. Futures markets were always related to agricultural and storable items, so that it was a departure. But it wasn't so much that departure that turned people away from it as it was the audacity it represented. The *Economist* wrote, "How dare we trade

the holy instruments of finance next to the Pork Belly pit."
That view was the accepted view of the establishment. New
York bankers would say, "What! Currency trading in Chicago?"
How ludicrous can you be! And indeed those were the symptoms. And those symptoms prevailed somewhat in our people
also. It wasn't just the innovation of trading financial instruments. That was part of it, but the main thing was that it was
an innovation that was being launched in Chicago while everyone in the world knew that the center of finance was either in
London or in New York. How dare we do this in Chicago! We,
who trade eggs and butter and onions and pork bellies and cattle, dare think of such a holy thing as finance. That's what was
so audacious about it in my view, and of course we proved all
the bankers wrong. We proved that the establishment was
wrong and that futures markets were an ideal mechanism for
finance. It didn't really matter to multinationals where the
markets existed. They could exist in London, in New York, and
in Chicago just as well. That's what happened then. It was both
an innovation and proof that finance fits the markets and you
can trade next to the cattle pits or next to the pork bellies pits.
It just doesn't matter. Electronic trading, on the other hand,
isn't truly the same kind of thing. No one says that an electronic trade for markets must be in New York, or electronic
trade can only be in New York. Nobody says that. The leap
here is to say whether or not an open-outcry environment can
be replaced by an electronic trade. And it is a much more difficult concept to accept, because the question of liquidity
comes into play. You can create liquidity in an open-outcry
environment, but can it be transferred to a screen? We were
not quite certain. The establishment says, "Wait a minute. I
grew up in open outcry. I didn't grow up in any other form. I

can't make money in any other form, I can't provide the services in any other form. Therefore I don't think it could create liquidity because without me it won't work." You can draw the comparison between these two events (the launch of financial futures in 1972 and the launch of electronic trading in 1992); there are these comparisons, but there's a huge difference in mentality. One is a resistance by the open-outcry establishment itself to accepting a different form of transaction architecture; the other is not our guys resisting it as much as the world around us saying, "This ain't for you. Finance is only for us refined folks in New York or in London.'" There is that kind of difference we faced.

Q. With the advent of electronics in at least a certain percentage of the exchanges, do you see possibly a tier level being set up with electronic trading? What I mean by that is, do you think that one day there might be a market maker at a retail level where there might be some type of an advantage to a professional trader who maybe owns a seat on the electronic exchange?

A. You can't yet come to a final conclusion about how this evolution that we are living through will end. There isn't anybody that smart. I have been in the forefront of taking our markets toward electronic trade even when everyone around me refused to accept its reality, including the former chairman of this exchange and others who now all have embraced it. But there was no embracing during only the early nineties. It was in 1995 when I wrote a piece called "Wake Up Call to the Exchanges," mentioning the fact that they have lost momentum in not moving to electronic trading. But having said that, I did not know and do not know today what the ultimate resolution will be. Here's what I do know. The Eurex market replaced the LIFFE market on the bund contract. It is totally electronic. There are no market makers. There's nothing but electronics at the Eurex, and it works famously well. The bund market today I believe is the largest volume trade, so it's hard for us to say that it can't work. It works! And there is no human intervention; there is no telephone intervention. On the other hand, in the United States there's still this bifurcated view. We have electronic trade with Globex and Project A, but the big markets and the big contracts are still traded on the floor in open-outcry fashion, and it's still problematic. I think that the large financial markets will in the very near future, and by that I mean within in a matter of 1 to 5 years, find themselves on an electronic screen. I think, however, there are some aspects of the markets that might not. Options have a difficult time with a screen methodology. That's now; perhaps 5 years from now someone will invent the way, the architecture and the program for options, that will work very well on the screen. So you can't be sure yet. On the other hand, if it is not invented, then perhaps options will maintain themselves on the floor in open-outcry architecture. Similarly in agriculture, there's been not nearly the pressure of movement toward electronics as there has been in financial markets. It's conceivable that agriculture will for the longest period remain in the open-outcry markets. It is also conceivable that some markets might find themselves in a compromised fashion where some of their products are on the screen and some not. Perhaps the far-out months due to the volatility are ones that don't have a great deal of liquidity, say in agriculture, and so they might very well be put on a screen, whereas the nearby ones that trade much more and in a more volatile fashion might stay on the open-outcry architecture. So what I am saying is that I don't want to overpredict. My prediction has been and still remains that the vast majority of our markets in finance will move to the screen. I have very little doubt about that. Then, the Eurex proved the question of liquidity beyond any doubt, so that I have no doubt about that. What I don't know is whether all the products will trade on the screen, whether there will be some hybrids, whether agriculture will, and whether options will.

There's another question, too. I think that the electronic screen offers itself as a laboratory for testing products much better then open outcry ever did. In open outcry there's a limitation of space; there's a limitation of people. It takes a great deal to build an infrastructure of a new market on the floor. Enormous amounts of resources go into it, both in human resources and in money resources. But with a screen, there's literally nothing to listing another product on that screen. It's limitless in space, and so you can leave it there. You don't need a community to gather around it right away.

It could develop over time; it could sit there for the longest period of time as a laboratory and as a pilot to determine whether in fact there's an audience for it; is there a user? So mainly you use the screen for that kind of laboratory, but then some would say "OK, let's assume you tried a new agricultural product, and we find after a period of time, in fact, there is universal usage. Maybe then we ought to put it into a pit and see if some locals will help generate some additional liquidity." There's nothing wrong with that kind of experiment. I wouldn't at all persuade anyone from that attempt. So what I'm saying is that there may be some aspects of open outcry that maybe in fact work hand in glove with electronic trading and I'm not opposed to that, nor am I wise enough to know how all this is going shake out. I just think, the direction is unmistakable, and if you ask me what it will be like 20 years from now, I think it most likely will all be on the screen.

Q. We, the futures industry, are introducing more and more electronic contracts one by one. Next month the Chicago Merc introduces the mini currency contract with electronics. It recently introduced the E-mini NASDAQ and of course the E-mini S&P. I'm going to compare this to the restaurant industry out in Milwaukee. Certainly a restaurant with a reputation will encourage people to travel from many places to go there. If a new restaurant opened next to it, you would not necessarily travel to that restaurant unless there was something outstanding about it. When many restaurants open on one street, people start calling it "restaurant row." What's starting to happen is people are actually going there because it's a restaurant community, and they're seeking out what restaurants are in that area and they're experimenting with different restaurants. With electronic trading, as the industry introduces new contracts, do you think that people are now going to the electronic arena and shopping just because it is available, just as they might go to restaurant row?

A. First of all, the restaurant example you use is better placed if you compare it with the shopping mall, and that's exactly why shopping malls have been very successful. Marshall Field's didn't mind if Nordstrom opened up next door to it because the combination attracted comparison buying and obviously it attracted shoppers who could go from one shop to another. So all these malls work on that principle and have since the 1960s. There's no question that there's a magnet effect that results from it all being in one environment. It almost is begging the question, because the point is that's the reason that I, for one, am urging us to have many products on the screen. I believe that, by doing that the user will have an easier time of it and would be attracted to that architecture.

It's clear that when a user has a complex trade that involves more than one instrument (most trades these days are very complex and do involve more than one instrument), he usually runs across a field of different markets. It could be bunds, against Euros, against whatnot. It is certainly more conducive to invite that user to trade when all of the instruments are before him on one screen. It's like a mall that attracts the best applications and comparisons and ease of shopping, so to speak; absolutely, it is exactly one of its main attractions. Obviously it's not the number one attraction. Its number one attraction is the efficiency of it, the number two attraction is the cost factor, and the number three is the ease factor that we're talking about.

Q. Take products such as the 30-year T-bond. Last year, the Chicago Board of Trade ran into a little bit of a scare from the Cantor Fitzgerald electronic threat, even if it didn't materialize too much. The CME has been licensed to use the trademark name "S&P" from McGraw-Hill as the franchise name. Do you think that exchanges themselves need to look at contracts like this and keep them exclusive?

A. It's not that easy to do. The S&P product, of course, is a proprietary product of Standard & Poor's. Although that question was an open issue for some time, actually it was resolved with the Dow case at the Board of Trade some years back. I had believed that it was a proprietary product from the start, as my book points out. I believed that because I'm a capitalist, and I feel that we should not use the name "Standard & Poor's" without paying them for it.

But having said that, the other kinds of things that we are trading are not proprietary. There's nothing proprietary about a U.S. bond, about a Eurodollar, or about a deutsche mark or a yen future, or anything like that. So it can't be protected in its form as it stands today. I think that the only patentable, in other words, trademark, methodology that could occur is if you intertwined it with a systems use. If, for instance, the way we launched yen futures and traded only through a mechanism that the Merc had invented, some special systems process, then you can go to the patent office and say, "OK, this is my trademark. This is my patent because you can only trade yen this way and anyone who wants to trade it this way can't do it." In its pure form as a currency, however, how can we stop anyone from trading that which isn't ours to start with? It's a much more complex thing, and I think that we have always been subject to this cannibalism once a product starts to trade.

The Eurodollar is the best example; everybody on earth has tried to trade Eurodollars. There is always sort of a centrifugal force in markets that occurs. Whoever creates the market first with enough magnetism and liquidity is the one who's going to succeed; all others will be little satellites by comparison. That sort of protects the originator, but not by actual law, not by actual trademark application. The Goldman Sachs Index is their index, they invented it, so it's a proprietary thing like Standard & Poor's.

Q. The catalyst for the industrial revolution was the printing press invented over 500 years ago by Gutenberg. The Internet seems to be the new catalyst of information and technology. What opportunities and dangers do you see that the actual exchanges and brokers are facing?

A. There's no doubt that it launched an entirely new world. Eventually the Internet changes the way we live, the way we work, the way we play; it changes every thing in life. All human endeavors have been changed by the digital revolution so to speak, and the Internet is only one part of it. It's a major innovation, and it will change everything we do in markets. There is no question in my mind that once we are released from the structure of a wired environment and instead can trade wireless, applications will change and methodologies will change. Where you trade changes, ideas change; everything changes. There's no imagination that is big enough to understand all that may occur in the coming century as a consequence of this Internet-transistor-digital world.

I know, for instance, that in one of my science fiction books I thought that we could all have an implant of a microchip in our brain, which would allow us to have mental transmissions between folks. There's no reason to believe that won't occur. Maybe it's not in the next 5 years, but it's not inconceivable. I wrote that in my book *The Tenth Planet* in 1984, so maybe somewhere in 20 years, in fact, that may occur. When and if such a thing occurs, it will allow us to trade through a mental process as well. There's no reason that we can't transmit orders that way. You can imagine the kind of transactions and the volume that this would invite. It's enormous, the potential that it unleashes.

Problems will occur as a result. Innovation has its constructive and destructive parts, so there's no doubt magnitudes of problems will occur that will be quite different than the ones being encountered today. We're already encountering problems in regulation. The Internet is very difficult to regulate, as the lawmakers are seeing. When you start to apply new market structures, that difficulty magnifies because you are now dealing with the possibility of a great deal of money and fraud, mistakes and errors, and whatnot. There is no doubt that the new world we've invented and entered will change everything and will include a whole host of new problems

Q. How do you feel about all this new technology?

A. Technology, I have said often, is the base cause of all human change. Anyone who ignores technological change is most likely going to be relegated to the waste bin. You cannot ignore technology. It changes and leads to change, and you must accept it.

Interview with Jack Sandner

Jack Sandner was appointed special policy advisor to the CME board of directors in January 1998, following his thirteenth year as chairman of the Chicago Mercantile Exchange, the longest-serving chairman in CME history. Sandner, who represents more than 2700 members and 86 member firms, was elected to a third consecutive 2-year term in 1996. Most recently under his leadership, the CME in 1995 embarked on an ambitious new initiative to trade products from the burgeoning emerging markets around the globe and established with overwhelming membership approval a new Growth and Emerging Markets (GEM) division of the exchange. Sandner continues to pursue new product and service initiatives, positioning the CME as the global financial services industry pacesetter for the 1990s and beyond. To that end, in 1995 U.S. Treasury Secretary Robert E. Rubin appointed him to the U.S. Advisory Commission on Financial Services.

Sandner, who joined the CME in 1971, has served continuously on its board of directors since 1977. He has served on and chaired scores of member committees. In 1978 he became president and CEO of RB&H Financial Services L.P., a futures commission merchant and clearing member firm of the CME.

Under Sandner's leadership, the CME developed the Eurodollar futures, the most actively traded derivatives product in the world; stock index futures and options, for which the Merc has become the world trading center; and Globex, the international after-hours electronic trading system, launched in 1992. In April 1993, he was appointed chairman of Globex. Recognized as an industry leader, he has testified frequently before Congress on the value and efficacy of futures risk management products. In December 1992, President Clinton invited Sandner to participate in an economic summit in Little Rock, where he served as the futures and options industry's sole representative.

Q. What is your outlook for electronic trading?

A. I think it's coming OK. I think this human cry that it's here, wake up, you're a dinosaur if you don't—all these kinds of sound bytes, they're really misplaced. I really believe that if an exchange is smart, it will prepare for this transition and understand the transition and, at the same time, try to figure out a model that creates value for the liquidity providers on the floor. It would be very stupid to make this transition and disenfranchise, say, 2000 capitalized liquidity providers, i.e., local traders. It just would be a stupid, stupid thing to do, and people don't see the scenario. To me it is just so naive. They go from it's either open outcry or electronic, and the model we're going to use is the model that appears to work. The model is one that an upstairs trader finds very, very comfortable to use. To me, that model does not work.

You need to do something that captures the upstairs trader electronically and, at the same time, excites and captures the mindset, call it the additive, of the downstairs liquidity provider because these are customers, if you will. They are quasi-customers. Let's put it that way, and they are not the pure retail customers. They provide the liquidity that allows people to enter and exit the marketplace. Every market is a little bit different, but it takes too long to dissect the marketplaces and the products and what kind of things they need. So the key is, if you're going to make that transition, which will happen, if you are smart, you'll take the best that you can take out of open outcry, in terms of liquidity, and then get somebody who is in a warm closet in Palo Alto to figure out what appeals to that mind. And that mind, at this point in time, is different from somebody from Goldman Sachs who sits upstairs and looks at his screen and makes a trade. These people, the liquidity providers, have never done that.

Q. Is there a way you can include the local trader so as to keep liquidity?

A. You take a front end and you develop some kind of a pulsating mechanism. Call it a Nintendo game or whatever. It's a trading vehicle that accommodates their personality, their profile, and you create an algorithm of some kind that gives them somewhat of a preferential position—and this sounds bad to a lot of people but it should be preferential—with certain requirements for that preferential position. They have a preferential position right now by being in the pit. They, more often than anyone else, will sell at the offer and buy at the bid. There is value in giving them preference so that they are there with the liquidity so that the institutions, when they're hedging asset allocations or even speculation, can enter and exit the market with the tighter bid and offers. So there's value in the quid pro quo in consideration for them.

The challenge, in my opinion, if people would buy into my concept, is that you retain that kind of expertise and develop that kind of a joystick world that they live in so that they don't leave and it creates value and opportunity for them. The other is easy. The Goldmans, the Morgans, the big trading institutions, or whoever—they're there; they're ready to do that. Right now the Euros, maybe they still like the voice broker, but if you showed them this seamless way of doing this, you bring the two parties together. The local market-making community and the institutions are brought together. You make that transition and you've done something that creates value and opportunity for the local trader.

What happens now in the debate is they say, "You will put me out of business if you turn to electronics." So you don't make the move until you're in crisis, and then it is too late to make a move. The preparation by the exchange is to build something to fill the dreams of the floor, which is a cyber-based floor that is a virtual trading front end for that community. One way you can do that, once you've started the front end, is by not giving that algorithm preferential to everybody. You give it to people in markets that have committed themselves to the markets they're in. I'm a Eurodollar person, you stay a Eurodollar person. If you want to trade yen you'll get the same algorithm that the upstairs traders get. So you've committed yourself to that market, and you've committed yourself to certain types of bids and offers that contain the preferential treatment on the screen. Now you haven't disenfranchised that liquidity provider; you haven't lost that community.

It also does something else for you. Since geography is irrelevant, someone will say, "My seat is worthless because my seat is about opportunity on the floor." Now you are talking about opportunity on the virtual trading machine. I'm talking about the local community now. That has been one of the sticking points—disenfranchising the 2000 people who vote. My feeling is the value and proposition for them is pretty extraordinary. There will be some who want it back, but if you do it this way and you put them through a very serious training campus, a virtual training campus, to learn to do these things slowly, during the transition what you have done is you have made geography now irrelevant. This will add so much value to that membership, that "market-making" membership, that it will be like an Internet play with the multiples. Here is why—because right now if you want to own that "market-making" local membership, to be on "the floor," you have to want to be in Chicago, want to come to 30 South Wacker or 141 West Jackson, and that's your life. So the constituency for that is very, very limited—very finite.

When geography is irrelevant and you have created that virtual pit, and you have created a market-making paradigm, that's different from the upstairs market-making paradigm, specifically for the market maker or liquidity provider. Geography is irrelevant because that front end for any particular market can be anywhere in the world, It could be in Tokyo. It could be in Indonesia. It could be in Santa Barbara. It could be in Chicago. But what has happened since geography now is irrelevant is that we do not have to come to 30 South Wacker. The potential constituency is no longer finite; it is virtually infinite. So the demand becomes Economics 101. The demand for that market-making membership increases exponentially. If you have demand for a seat on the floor to trade and you created something that's as exciting off the floor for that trade, and the person can do that without moving to Chicago, and without going to 30 South Wacker, it's clear that the potential participant and demand for that particular membership or vehicle increases dramatically. And so the value of the membership goes up dramatically.

Moreover, as a plus, the exchange will be filled up and the market will have liquidity providers. If the exchange wants to, it can turn the key and split the memberships just like we've done in the past with the IOM. We gave the members a seat for $100 back in 1972 that is now worth $30,000. Now, at the pleasure of the board, if the demand gets up so high, you can open memberships up a little bit. By opening it up, you are continuing to create value for the person who owns the seat, but you bring more traders in to create more liquidity. So it's like an exponential equation that just keeps adding value. At the same time, you are offering risk management services and asset allocation to all the institutions' liquidity, so it is 1 and 1 equals 3.

Q. There is talk that the Merc might go public. How do you feel about this?

A. If we're going to make that transition in a very comfortable way, we have to do those kinds of things and I think we can do them. The demutualization is critical because it gives you the latitude to be very flexible and do a lot of things. When you become a for-profit organization, you do things differently. You unlock the equity for the member that you're demutualizing and you can create a currency to allow you to make other deals with strategic partners. You now have a stock. So you can make strategic alliances with technology companies and with information companies, and that really adds strategic value to your template and your plan.

At the same time we are in the new economy where it's an Internet type economy in an information technology–driven economy. So we've got to explore that information and technology world to capitalize on what's happened. Clearly geography is irrelevant. We also have entered into a new world. Eight or nine years ago, the population was X in the world, and there were communists and socialists. Then the wall came tumbling down. Communism is bad, socialism is bad, and the world now is embracing capitalism in free markets. It still has a way to go, but now what we have done is taken 2 billion people who had been locked in the prison of socialism and unlocked those prison gates and they're coming out. They are consumers in the free market. Potentially, at first, some will starve on the way to a free-market society. But as it sorts itself out, what we've done is increased the consuming world, the free-market world, by huge multiples. So what happens when you've done that is risk management becomes a much more needed facility for institutions because of the products in the world and globalization and because the information technology makes the world borderless. There are no borders and you've got all the consumers out there. It's just a huge tectonic plate movement that starts to come together.

At the same time that the world is embracing free markets, you have another culture that is developing. And the culture that is developing is a culture of those who believe in risk management. The pension funds, the General Motors, they're all using these kinds of risk management vehicles. Also, there's a speculative will of improving your lot that will be seen like we've never seen before. Some people will say speculation is bad, but that's bull. Speculation is what drives incentives, and some people lose, some people don't, but it drives incentives to produce and improve your lot in life. It serves an unbelievable function of providing liquidity for the institutions that manage risk. So in a sense, it securitizes the whole marketplace. So you've got risk management that will grow dramatically, and for that there is no better tool than derivatives.

In addition to the speculative culture that will grow dramatically, we will have one other thing that the world is telling us to have in this culture, and that is transaction security. Remember the long-term capital situation? All these situations point to transaction security, especially if you operate on a global basis, because on that scale it gets even more uncertain. Is someone going to pay from this venue to that venue? So transaction security is going to be part of that culture. If you take that blueprint and ask students taking an exam in college to explain in a short paragraph the key ingredients of the Chicago Mercantile Exchange, the A students would say risk management, speculation, and transaction security clearing. Those are the three separate items. There are other things, but those three items are key. So that would get an A on an exam. We are what the world is going toward, and the world is growing geometrically in that venue.

Q. What is the Merc going to do to attract this business?

A. It's now up to us to capitalize on the globalization by giving traders around the world the arteries through which to come to this exchange. I believe open outcry is a wonderful, wonderful system, but we have to ask ourselves, can we develop a system electronically that is as good as or better than open outcry and at the same time create value and not disenfranchise the liquidity provider? I believe that's the challenge, and I think we can meet that challenge. If we do, we win the world. And products will just proliferate and come to our exchange with all sorts of risk management products, and there will only be a couple of exchanges that will be "the exchanges in the world." They will be in different time zones. There will probably be one huge exchange in the United States, and hopefully that will be us. So I believe electronic trading is not here and now in the United States. Eurex is not a good example. LIFFE is not a good example. In my opinion I can give you all the arguments why this is the way you've got to do it. Look what Eurex has done, and that's a whole different paradigm for trade. They have the big German banks, their nationalism, and their commitment to the bund; and their open-outcry system wasn't anything like the depth that we have.

Q. What do you see as the perfect electronic system for the Merc?

A. You could theoretically build a seamless, paperless order entry system with execution at the end and keep open outcry. But you don't do that if two things happen: If we can develop an electronic system that doesn't disenfranchise the local trading liquidity provider, we've hit the grand slam home run because of its exponential increase in terms of value for everybody. Then the membership would break the doors down, because they would say, "I'm not disenfranchised now. The value of my seat is going to go way, way up. I can trade electronically with a quality of life that's quite a bit different from hanging around the floor." Quite a different mindset than it is now.

The question is now, "Why should I vote for something like that when I'd lose my job? I'm out of business." You've got to show them that you're not out of business. As a matter of fact, adaptation is very easy. You are not a monkey; you can adapt. That's a win-win for everybody, and I think when we do that, that's where it will go. Right now just to turn the switches and say you're all electronic, it would be the most irresponsible thing to do, and we would fall on our face. And so would any other exchange in the United States of America that has a strong clearing base through its market-making system. Eurex is not the right example. It's a sign, but it's not a good example, so we're not ready yet for that. We are the only exchange in the United States that is preparing a clicks and brick scenario. We have the E-mini trading right next to the big S&P. One is fueling the other. There's an arbitrage; there's financial engineering that's going on. That is a safety net for everybody, and it's flourishing. And now the adaptation is happening, and we are queuing up to get the screens to trade the E-minis as a member from the floor. Traders want to be on the floor, and we didn't have the bandwidth, and we didn't think there would be that much demand. We're probably 80 deep still applying for NASDAQ screens, E-mini screens, and you see what's happened by doing that. Look what happened to the Dow contract at the Board of Trade. We're trading 6 to 1 what they are trading, and that is a terrible, terrible failure. Unfortunately, Dow's a wonderful company—Peter Khan the chairman and all the people that were involved—and they are wonderful, wonderful, thoughtful people. But it was a failed proposition, and we did it electronically and did it with a safety net Because you can lean on the big open-outcry price discovery system that was up a natural seven or royal flush for us. There was no way the Dow could ever compete with that. So that now is an adaptation that the people see, recognize, and love. The fear for people making the transitions gets less and less and less. What we must do is improve on that model of trade for the local who is licensed to use the machine as a member in a floor-type virtual setting, but we may not do that. I think if we did that, we would unlock the door to opportunity that is unlike any other opportunity ever before in our exchange.

Conclusion

Anyone who spends time around traders will eventually hear every excuse for why a trade went wrong. The interesting notion in all this is that the excuses are usually right on target. What is often lost in the telling is not the excuse itself, but the pathology that gives meaning to the excuse. If a common thread weaves through the "should've, could've, and would've" of trading, it is the readiness of traders to identify the external forces that caused a good trade to go bad.

On the other hand, there are few public acknowledgments of the internal psychological forces that consign trades to the loss column. Individuals who shoot from the hip, chase markets, or take a shot are gamblers, not traders, and they can always lay blame elsewhere. They are all pathology and no plan. In the same sense, these individuals lack the patience, willpower, or discipline to study themselves and understand who they are (an E or an I). It is how you react to disruption and disappointment, your willingness to make adjustments, and your ability to view the markets dispassionately that will determine whether you are on the path to becoming a competent trader, one who acknowledges every facet of trading as integral to the whole.

Developing a facility with the tools of trading is the easy part. Just about anyone can develop a good working knowledge of technical analysis in a reasonably short time. The indicators we have reviewed provide a primer for further study. It is not the difficulty of the material that is the real hindrance in learning to use the indicators. It's the murky pathology that resides within each trader.

Traders directed by their emotions will always be inclined to worry that they don't know enough. We call it the "never enough indicator syndrome." Developing your trading skills in their fullest sense is inextricably linked to your psychological profile. None of us ever know enough. Many of us don't know how to adequately use that which we understand. There isn't a quiz you must pass to qualify you as a competent trader. The markets qualify you every day. That we miss something in the market structure, in the analytical overlay that guides us or even an obvious fundamental, isn't predictive of whether we are competent traders. We all miss something. The real power is in learning from those misses and making the learning process indispensable to your development as a trader.

We talk to both experienced and novice traders from around the world every trading day. Over the years the stories and laments we hear are universal in their application. The Internet has given all of us access to more data than we can reasonably use while fostering a search for the secret of trading. There are no secrets. There is no holy grail. The real work in preparation is diligence in converting information to knowledge within a system, methodology, or plan, not in gathering more and more information. Information and analysis are not ends in and of themselves. And the success in executing that system, methodology, or plan begins with a clear vision and understanding of who you are.

FUTURES and DERIVATIVES EXCHANGES

The follow list of futures and derivatives exchanges illustrates the breadth of the global market for futures trading. Alliances and mergers are taking place almost daily, reflecting the growing influence of electronic networks.

Argentina

Buenos Aires Futures Market
Bouchard 454, 5, (1106), Buenos Aires. Argentina
(54)1311-4716; fax (54)1-312-3180
e-mail: Info-matba@matba.corn.ar

Australia

Australian Stock Exchange, Derivatives
A division of the Australian Stock Exchange Ltd.
20 Bond St., Sydney, NSW2000, Australia
61-2-227-0000; fax 61-2-251-5525
Options on 56 equities and 3 indexes

Sydney Futures Exchange (SFE)

30-32 Grosvenor St., Sydney. NSW 2000. Australia

61-2-9256-0555; fax 61-2-9256-0666

Austria

Wiener Borse AG

A-1014 Vienna, Strauchgasse 1-3, P.O. Box 192

43-1-531-65-0; fax 43-1-532-9740

e-mail: info@wbag.at

Belgium

Belgian Futures and Options Exchange (BELFOX)

Palais de la Bourse, Rue Henry Maus, 2. 1000 Brussels,
    Belgium

32-2-512-80-40; fax 32-2-513-83-42

Brazil

Bolsa de Mercadorias & Futuros (BM&F)

The Commodities & Futures Exchange, Praca Antonio
    Prado, 48, São Paulo, SP, Brazil

01010-901. 55-11-3119-2000

Canada

Montreal Exchange (ME)

The Stock Exchange Tower, P.O. Box 61, 800, Victoria
    Square, Montreal, Quebec H4Z 1A9 Canada

(514) 871-2424; fax (514) 871-3531

Toronto Futures Exchange (TFE)

Two First Canadian Place, The Exchange Tower, Toronto,
    Ontario M5X 1J2 Canada

(416) 947-4487; fax (416) 947-4272

Toronto Stock Exchange (TSE)
Two First Canadian Place, The Exchange Tower, Toronto,
    Ontario M5X 1J2 Canada
(416) 947-4700; fax (416) 947-4272

Vancouver Stock Exchange (VSE)
609 Granville St., Stock Exchange Tower, Vancouver,
    B.C. V7Y 1H1 Canada
(604) 689-3334; fax (604) 688-6051

The Winnipeg Commodity Exchange (WCE)
500 Commodity Exchange Tower, 360 Main St.,
    Winnipeg, Manitoba R3C 3Z4 Canada
(204) 925-5000; fax (204) 943-5448

Chile

Santiago Stock Exchange
La Bolsa 64, Casilla 123-D, Santiago, Chile
56-2-698-2001; 56-2-695-8077; fax 56-2-672-8046

China

Beijing Commodity Exchange (BCE)
306 Chenyun Building, No. 8 Beichen East Road,
    Chaoyang District, Beijing 100101 China
86-1-6492-8347; 86-1-6493-3183; fax 86-1-6499-3365;
    86-1-6493-3183

Denmark

FUTOP Market—Copenhagen Stock Exchange and the
FUTOP Clearing Center Copenhagen Stock Exchange
Nikolaj Plads 6, Box 1040, DK-1007 Copenhagen,
Denmark
45-33-93-3366; fax 45-33-12-8613

Finland

Finnish Options Exchange Ltd.
Erottajankatu 11, SF-00130, Helsinki, Finland
35-8-9-680-3410; fax 35-8-9-604-442

Helsinki Securities and Derivatives Exchange (HEX)
Keskuskatu 7, P.O. Box 926, FIN-00101 Helsinki, Finland
35-8-9-616-671; fax 35-8-9-6166-7366

France

Marche a Terme International de France (MATIF)
115 rue Reaumur, 75002 Paris, France
33-1-4028-8282; fax 33-1-4028-8001; Telex: 218-362

Marche des Options Negociables de Paris (MONEP)
MONEP SA, 39, rue Cambon, 75001 Paris, France
33-1-49-27-18-00; fax 33-1-49-27-18-23; Telex: 214-538 F

Germany

Eurex Frankfurt
Postal address: 60284 Frankfurt
Street address: Boersenplatz 7-11, 60313 Frankfurt,
Germany
49-69-2101-0; fax 49-69-2101-2005; Telex: 4175 953 dtb d

Greece

Athens Stock Exchange

Hong Kong

Hong Kong Futures Exchange Ltd. (HKFE)
5/F, Asia Pacific Finance Tower, Citibank Plaza,
   3 Garden Rd., Hong Kong
852-2531-5056; fax 852-2824-4438

The Stock Exchange of Hong Kong (SEHK)
1/F, One & Two Exchange Square, Central, Hong Kong
852-2522-1122; fax 852-2530-2911

Hungary

Budapest Commodity Exchange
H-1373, P.O. Box 495, H-1134 Budapest,
   Robert Karoly krt. 61-65
36-1-269-8571; fax 36-1-269-8575

Budapest Stock Exchange
H-1052 Budapest. Deak F. u. 5. Hungary
36-1-117-5226; fax 36-1-118-1737

India

National Stock Exchange of India

Israel

The Tel Aviv Stock Exchange Ltd. (TASE)
54 Ahad Haam St., Tel Aviv, 65202, Israel
972-3-567-7411; fax 972-3-510-5379; 972-3-566-1822

Italy

Italian Stock Exchange
Piazza degli Affari. 6. 20123, Milan, Italy
39-2-724-261; fax 39-2-72-00-43-33

Japan

Chubu Commodity Exchange (C-COM)
2-15, Nishiki, 3-chome, Naka-ku, Nagoya 460, Japan
81-52-951-2171; fax 81-52-961-6407

Kanmon Commodities Exchange
1-5 Nabe-machi, Shimonoseki, Yamaguchi 750-0006,
    Japan
81-832-31-1313; fax 81-832-23-1947

Kansai Commodities Exchange (KANEX)
1-10-14 Awaza, Nishi-ku, Osaka 550, Japan
81-6-531-7931; fax 81-6-541-9343

Nagoya Stock Exchange (NSE)
3-17 Sakae, 3-chome, Naka-ku, Nagoya 460, Japan
81-52-262-3172; fax 81-52-241-1527

Osaka Mercantile Exchange
5-28 Kyutaro-machi, 2-chome, Chuo-ku, Osaka
    541-0056, Japan
81-6-244-2191; fax 81-6-244-2194

Osaka Securities Exchange (OSE)
8-16, Kitahama, 1-chome, Chuo-ku, Osaka 541, Japan
81-6-229-8643; fax 81-6-231-2639

Tokyo Commodity Exchange (TOCOM)
l4th Floor, S. Wing, Riverside Yomiuri Bldg.,
    36-2 Nihonbashi-Hakozakicho, Chuoku, Tokyo 103,
    Japan
81-3-3661-9191; fax 81-3-3661-7568

Tokyo Grain Exchange (TGE)
12-5 Nihonbashi Kakigara-cho, 1-chome, Chuo-ku,
    Tokyo 103-0014, Japan
81-3-3668-9317; fax 81-3-3661-4564

Tokyo International Financial Futures Exchange
    (TIFFE)
1-3-1 Marunouchi, Chiyoda-ku, Tokyo 100, Japan
81-3-5223-2400; fax 81-3-5223-2450

Tokyo Stock Exchange (TSE)
2-1 Nihombashi-Kabuto-Cho, Chuo-ku, Tokyo 103-8220,
    Japan
81-3-3666-0141; fax 81-3-3663-0625; Telex: 02522759

Yokohama Commodities Exchange
1 Yamashita-sho, Naka-ku, Yokohama, Kanagawa,
    231-0023, Japan
81-45-641-1341; fax 81-45-641-1346

Korea

Korea Stock Exchange
33. Yoido-dong, Youngdeungpo-ku, Seoul 150-010 Korea
(82) 2-3774-9000; fax (82) 2-761-3769
e-mail: futures@kse.or.kre

Malaysia

Kuala Lumpur Commodity Exchange (KLCE)

Fourth Floor, Citypoint, Dayabumi Complex, Jalan
Sultan Hishamuddin, P.O. Box 11260, 50740 Kuala
Lumpur, Malaysia

(60) 3-293-6822; fax (60) 3-274-2215; Telex: MA 31472
KLCE

e-mail: klce@po.jaring.my

Kuala Lumpur Options and Financial Futures Exchange
(KLOFFE)

10th Floor. Citypoint, Chase Perdana, Off Jalan
Semantan, Damansara Heights, 50490 Kuala
Lumpur, Malaysia

(60) 3-293-8199; fax (60) 3-253-2911/255-3207

e-mail: kloffe@kloffe.com.my

Netherlands

Amsterdam Exchanges (AEX)

Postbus 19163, 1000 GD Amsterdam, The Netherlands

31-20-550-4444; fax 31-20-550-4950

New Zealand

New Zealand Futures and Options Exchange (NZFOE)

P.O. Box 6734, Wellesley St., 10th Level, Stock
Exchange Centre, Auckland, New Zealand

64-9-309-8308; fax 64-9-309-8817

Norway

Oslo Stock Exchange (OSLO)

P.O. Box 460, Sentrum, N-0105 Oslo, Norway

47-22-34-17-00; fax 47-22-41-65-90; Telex: 77242

Peru

Lima Stock Exchange (Bolsa de Valores de Lima)

Portugal

Bolsa de Derivados do Porto (BDP)

Av. da Boavista, 3433, 4100 Porto, Portugal

(35) 1-2-618-58-58; fax (35) 1-2-618-58-97

Romania

Sibiu Monetary Financial and Commodities Exchange
(BMFMS)

Plata 1 Decembrie 1918, No. 69, 2400 Sibiu, Romania

40-69-211-153; fax 40-69-211-799

Singapore

Singapore Commodity Exchange Ltd.

111 North Bridge Rd. #23-04/05, Peninsula Plaza,
Singapore 179098

(65) 338-5600; fax (65) 338-9116; (65) 338-9640;
(65) 338-9676

Singapore International Monetary Exchange Ltd.
  (SIMEX)
1 Raffles Place, No. 07-00, OUB Centre, Singapore
  048616
(65) 535-7382; fax (65) 535-7282
e-mail: simex@pacific.net.s

SIMEX America Ltd., 10 E. 40th St., Suite 4205,
  New York, NY 10016
(212) 481-8080; fax (212) 481-7373

South Africa

South African Futures Exchange (SAFEX)
105 Central St., Houghton Estate 2198, P.O. Box 95709,
  Grant Park 2051, Republic of South Africa
(27) 11-728-5960; fax (27) 11-728-5970

Spain

Madrid Stock Exchange

MEFF Renta Fija (MEFF-RF)
Via Laietana, 58, 08003, Barcelona, Spain
34-3-412-1128; fax 34-3-268-4769

MEFF Renta Variable (MEFF-RV)
Torre Picasso, Planta 26, 28020 Madrid, Spain
34-1-585-0800; fax 34-1-571-9542

Sweden

OM Stockholm AB (OMS)
Norrlandsgatan 31 SE-105 78 Stockholm, Sweden
(46) 8-405-6000; fax (46) 8-405-6001

Stockholm Stock Exchange

Switzerland

Eurex Zurich AG
Selnaustrasse 30, Postfach CH-8021 Zurich, Switzerland
(41) 1-229-2999; fax (41) 1-229-2254

Taiwan

Taiwan Stock Exchange

Thailand

Thailand Stock Exchange

United Kingdom

International Petroleum Exchange of London Ltd. (IPE)
International House, 1 St. Katharine's Way, London
    E1 9UN, United Kingdom
44-171-481-0643; fax 44-171-481-8485
web site: www.energylive.com

London International Financial Futures and Options
    Exchange (LIFFE)
Cannon Bridge, London EC4R 3XX, United Kingdom
44-171-623-0444; fax 44-171-588-3624; Telex: 893893

London Metal Exchange (LME)
56 Leadenhall Street, London EC3A 2BJ, United Kingdom
44-171-264-5555; fax 44-171-680-0505; Telex: 8951367

The London Securities and Derivatives Exchange
    (OMLX)
107 Cannon St., London EC4N 5AD, United Kingdom
44-171-283-0678; fax 44-171-815-8508

United States

American Stock Exchange (AMEX)
(Part of the NASDAQ-AMEX Market Group)
Derivative Securities, 86 Trinity Place, New York, NY
    10006
(212) 306-1000; fax (212) 306-1802

Chicago Board Options Exchange (CBOE)
400 S. LaSalle St., Chicago, IL 60605
(312) 786-5600; (800) 678-4667; fax (312) 786-7409;
(312) 786-7413

Chicago Board of Trade (CBOT)
141 W. Jackson Blvd, Chicago, IL 60604-2994
(312) 435-3500; fax (312) 341-31306

Chicago Board of Trade Clearing Corp.
141 W. Jackson Blvd., Suite 1460, Chicago, IL 60604
(312) 786-5700; fax (312) 341-0293

Chicago Stock Exchange (CHX)
One Financial Place, 440 S. LaSalle St., Chicago, IL
    60605-1070
(312) 663-2222; fax (312) 663-2396

Chicago Mercantile Exchange (CME)
30 S. Wacker Drive, Chicago, IL 60606
(312) 930-1000; fax (312) 930-3439
Includes Globex: (312) 910-2397; fax (312) 930-8219

Coffee, Sugar & Cocoa Exchange Inc.
(A subsidiary of the Board of Trade of the City of New
    York Inc.)
4 World Trade Center, New York, NY 10048
(212) 742-6000, (800) 433-4348: fax (212) 748-4321

Kansas City Board of Trade (KCBT)
4800 Main St., Suite 303, Kansas City, MO 64112
(816) 753-7500; (800) 821-5228; fax (816) 753-3944;
    hotline (800) 821-4444

MidAmerica Commodity Exchange (MidAm)
(An affiliate of the Chicago Board of Trade)
141 W. Jackson Blvd., Chicago, IL 60604
(312) 341-3000; fax (312) 341-3027

Minneapolis Grain Exchange (MGE)
400 S. Fourth St., Minneapolis, MN 55415
(612) 321-7101; fax (612) 339-1155
e-mail. mgex@ix.netcom.com

The Board of Trade of the City of New York Inc.
(See Coffee, Sugar & Cocoa Exchange above or New
York Cotton Exchange below.)

New York Cotton Exchange (NYCE)
(A subsidiary of the Board of Trade of the City of New
York Inc.)
Four World Trade Center, New York, NY 10048
(212) 742-5054; fax (212) 742-5026

FINEX in New York:
(212) 742-5021; fax (212) 742-5026

FINEX in Europe: Dublin Exchange Facility,
International Financial Services Centre, Dublin 1,
Ireland
(353) 1-607-4000; fax (353) 1-607-4064

Citrus Associates of the NYCE Inc.
NYFE: (212) 748-1248; (800) 843-6933;
fax (212) 742-5026

New York Mercantile Exchange
(Includes NYMEX and COMEX divisions)
One North End Ave., World Financial Center, New York,
NY 10282-1101
(212) 299-2000; fax (212) 301-4700
e-mail: exchangeinfo@nymex.com

New York Stock Exchange (NYSE)
11 Wall St., New York, NY 10005
(212) 656-2804

Pacific Stock Exchange (PSE)
301 Pine St., San Francisco, CA 94104
(415) 393-4000; fax (415) 393-5964

Philadelphia Stock Exchange (PHLX)/Philadelphia
    Board of Trade (PBOT)
1900 Market St., Philadelphia. PA 19103
(215) 496-5000; (800) 843-7459; fax (215) 496-5653
e-mail: info@phlx.com

Venezuela
Caracas Stock Exchange

Glossary

A

Actuals—Physical products bought and sold in the spot market.

Adaptive filter—A systematic means of continuously updating the weighting of past prices for smoothing or forecasting purposes.

Advance-decline line—Each day's declining issues are subtracted from that day's advancing issues. The difference is added to (subtracted from, if negative) a running sum, Failure of this line to confirm a new high is a sign of weakness. Failure of this line to confirm a new low is a sign of strength.

Allowances—The discounts (premiums) allowed the buyer for the grades or locations of a commodity lower (higher) than the par or basis grade or location specified in the futures.

Alpha-beta trend channel—The alpha-beta trend channel study uses the standard deviation of price variation to establish two trend lines, one above and one below the moving average of a price field. This creates a channel (band) where the great majority of price field values will occur.

Approved delivery facility—Any bank, stockyard, mill, store, warehouse, plant, elevator, or any other institution that is authorized by the exchange for delivery of exchange contracts.

Arbitrage—Simultaneous purchases or sales of the same basic contract in different markets to profit from discrepancies in prices between those markets.

Area pattern—After a stock's or commodity's upward or downward trend has stalled, the sideways movement in price which follows forms a pattern. Some of these patterns may have predictive value. Examples of these patterns are head and shoulders, triangles, pennants, flags, wedges, and broadening formations.

At the market—An order to buy or sell at the best price obtainable at the time the order is received.

B

Basis—The difference between the spot price and the price of the futures.

Basis grade—The commodity grade used as the contract standard.

Bear—A person who believes prices will move lower.

Bear market—A market in which prices are declining.

Bid—An offer to purchase at a specified price.

Bollinger bands—Trading bands plotted above and below a

simple moving average. The standard deviation of closing prices for a period equal to the moving average employed is used to determine the band width. This causes the bands to tighten in quiet markets and loosen in volatile markets. The bands can be used to determine overbought and oversold levels, locate reversal areas, project targets for market moves, and determine appropriate stop levels. The bands are used in conjunction with indicators such as RSI MACD histogram, CCI, and rate of change. Divergences between Bollinger bands and other indicators show potential action points. As a general guideline, look for buying opportunities.

Break—A rapid and sharp decline in price.

Broker—A firm or person that handles the execution of all trades.

Bull—A person who believes prices will rise.

Bull market—A market in which prices are rising.

Buy in—Purchasing a contract to cover or close out a short position.

Buy on close—To buy at the end of the trading session at a price within the closing range.

Buy on open—To buy at the beginning of the trading session at a price within the opening range.

C

Call—An option that gives the owner the right to buy a security or commodity at a predetermined price within a given time period.

Candlestick charts—A charting method originally developed in Japan. The high and low are described as shadows and plotted as a single line. The price range between the open and close is plotted as a rectangle on the single line. If the close of the day is above the open, the body of the rectangle is white. If the close of the day is below the open, the body of the rectangle is black.

Car—A loose, quantitative term typically used to describe a contract, e.g., "car of bellies." Derived from when quantities of the product specified on a contract often corresponded closely to the quantity carried in a railroad car.

Carrying broker—A member of a futures exchange, usually a futures commission merchant, through whom another broker or customer elects to "clear" all or some of his or her trades.

Carrying charges—The cost of storing a physical commodity over a period of time. Includes insurance and interest on the invested funds as well as other incidental costs.

Cash commodity—The actual physical commodity, as distinguished from a futures contract for that commodity.

Cash market—A market for immediate delivery and payment of commodities.

Certified stocks—Quantities of commodities designated and certified for delivery by an exchange under its trading and testing regulations at delivery points specified and approved by the exchange.

Chaikin oscillator—An oscillator created by subtracting a 10-day exponential moving average from a 3-day exponential moving average of the accumulation distribution line.

Channel—A term used in charting, it allows the user to draw parallel lines connecting the low points and the high points. It can be ascending or descending.

Clear—To be verified and guaranteed.

Clearinghouse—An adjunct to a futures exchange through which transactions executed on the floor of the exchange are settled. Also charged with assuring the proper conduct of delivery procedures and the adequate financing of the trading.

Clearing member—A member of the clearinghouse or association. All trades of a non-clearing member must be registered and eventually settled through a clearing member.

Clerk—A member's employee who has been registered to work on the trading floor as a phone person or runner.

Close—A short period at the end of the trading session during which the closing price range is established. Sometimes referred to as the "closing price."

Closing range (or range)—The closing price (or price range) recorded during the period designated as the official close.

Commercial stocks—Commodities in storage in public and private elevators or warehouses at important markets and afloat in vessels or barges in harbors and ports.

Commission—The fee charged by a broker to a customer when a transaction is made.

Commitment—Made when a trader assumes the obligation to accept or make delivery by entering into a futures contract.

Commodity channel index (CCI) A timing system that is best applied to commodity contracts that have cyclical or seasonal tendencies. The CCI does not determine the length of cycles. It is designed to detect when such cycles begin and end through the use of a statistical analysis that incorporates a moving average and a divisor reflecting both the possible and actual trading ranges.

Commodity Exchange Act—A federal act passed in 1936 establishing the Commodity Exchange Authority and placing futures trading in a wide range of commodities under the regulation of the government.

Commodity Futures Trading Commission (CFTC). Established in 1975, responsible for regulation of all U.S. futures and options trading.

Commodity pool—An enterprise in which funds contributed by a number of persons are combined for purposes of trading futures or options for profits.

Commodity trading advisor (CTA)—A person who advises others about the value or advisability of buying or selling futures contracts or options or who trades on the customer's behalf. A CTA trades with other people's money. Must be registered with the CFTC.

Contango—A condition that exists when the front-month prices are lower than the back-month prices, This is normal for most markets, because back months include carrying costs (interest, storage, etc.).

Contract—A unit of trading in futures, specifying the quantity and quality of the commodity. Also, the actual bilateral agreement between buyer and seller in a futures transaction.

Contract grade—That grade of commodity that has been officially approved by an exchange as deliverable in settlement of a futures contract.

Contract month—The month in which futures contracts may be satisfied by making or accepting delivery. Also called "delivery month."

Cost and freight (C&F). Paid to move a commodity to a port of destination and included in quoted price.

Cost, insurance, and freight (CIF). Paid to move a commodity to a port of destination and included in the quoted price.

Cover—The purchase of futures to offset a previously established position.

Crop year—The period of time from one harvest or storage cycle to the next: varies with each commodity.

Cross-rate—In foreign exchange, the price of one currency in terms of another currency in the market of a third country.

D

Day order—Orders that are placed for execution, if possible, during only one trading session. If the order cannot be executed that day, it is automatically canceled.

Day trading—Refers to establishing and liquidating the same position or positions within a trading day.

Deferred futures—Futures contracts that expire during the more distant months.

Delivery—The tender and receipt of an actual commodity, warehouse receipt, or other negotiable instrument covering such commodity in settlement of a futures contract.

Demand aggregate—A quantity that represents current volume as well as open interest. A rise in price, coupled with rising volume and open interest figures, is considered a bullish indicator. Interpretations are made with respect to the relationship between the movement of volume, open interest, and price.

Demand index—A leading indicator that represents a combination of volume and price data in a manner that indicates a change in price trend. It is designed so that at the very least it is a coincidental indicator, never a lagging one. The calculation of this index is relatively complex. This analysis is based on observing that volume tends to peak before prices peak, both in the commodity and stock markets.

Detrend—A system that filters out the shorter-term trends so that cyclical movement that is not readily apparent in most trend charts can be observed.

Devaluation—A formal "official" decrease in the value of a country's currency, that is typically initiated by that country.

Discount—Less than par. If a future delivery is selling at a discount to the spot delivery, then it is selling for a lower price than the spot price.

Discretionary account—An account over which an individual or organization, other than the person in whose name the account is carried, exercises trading authority or control. Typically, used by brokers or CTAs.

E

Elliott wave—A theory that provides an overall view of market movement that helps explain why and where certain chart patterns develop. The three major aspects of wave analysis are pattern, time, and ratio. The basic Elliott pattern consists of a 5-wave uptrend followed by a 3-wave correction. Each "leg" of a wave in turn consists of smaller waves. The Elliott wave theory can be used to define where the market currently is in relation to a longer cycle but is usually too unreliable for short-term trading.

Equity—The residual dollar value of a futures trading account, assuming it's liquidated at the going market price.

Eurodollar—U.S. dollar deposits held abroad. Holders may include individuals, companies, banks, and central banks.

Evening up—Buying or selling to offset an existing market position.

Exchange for physicals (EFPs)—A technique in which a physical commodity position is traded for a futures position.

Exchange rate—The "price" of one currency stated in terms of another currency.

Expiration—The date or month in which the contract expires or is no longer traded.

Ex-pit transactions—Trades executed, for certain technical purposes, in a location other than the regular exchange trading pit.

F

Fibonacci ratio—The relationship between two numbers in the Fibonacci sequence. The sequence for the first three numbers is 0.618, 1.0, and 1.618. In general terms the Fibonacci series is 1, 1, 2, 3, 5, 8, 13, 21, 34, 55, 89, etc.

Floor broker—An exchange member who executes orders for the account of one or more clearing members.

Floor trader—An exchange member who executes trades for his or her own account or for an account that is controlled by the trader. Also referred to as a "local."

Foreign exchange—Foreign currency. Often referred to as "Forex" or "interbank market."

Forward—In the future.

Forward market—Informal (non-exchange) trading of contracts of future delivery. Contracts for forward delivery are "personalized"; i.e., delivery time and amount are determined by the customer.

Futures—A term designating the standardized contracts covering the sale of commodities for future delivery on a futures exchange.

Futures commission merchant (FCM)—A firm or person that is engaged in soliciting or accepting and handling orders for the purchase or sale of commodities for future delivery on, or subject to the rules of, a futures exchange and that, in connection with such solicitation or acceptance of orders, accepts any money or securities to margin any resulting trades or contracts. Must be licensed under the Commodity Exchange Act. All FCMs are not necessarily clearing members of an exchange. In that case, orders are handled by a clearing member on an omnibus basis.

G

Gann square—The Gann square is based on the theories of W. D. Gann, who gained some prominence as an astrologer and numerologist and believed that natural external forces influenced the markets and their cycles. He used various numerical sequences such as squaring, doubling, and tripling of numbers, as well as Fibonacci numbers. The Gann square system is based on a commodity or stock's extreme low or high price during a given period. When a commodity reaches a particular price level in a square it tells you the next probable price peak or valley. The predictive price levels are considered to be more reliable if they are extrapolated from Gann square values along one of the major axes of the Gann square. The Gann square is generated from a central value, normally an all-time or cyclical high or low. If a low is used, the numbers are increased by a constant amount to generate the Gann square. If a high is used, the numbers are decreased during the square generation.

Give-up—An order that at the request of the customer is credited to a brokerage house that has not performed the execution service.

Good 'til canceled (GTC) An order to a broker to buy or sell at a fixed price. The order holds until executed or canceled.

Grading certificate—A paper setting forth the quality of a physical commodity as determined by authorized inspectors or graders.

H

Head and shoulder pattern—A reversal pattern that is one of the more common and reliable patterns. It is composed of a rally that ends a fairly extensive advance. It is followed by a reaction on less volume. This is the left shoulder. The head is composed of a rally up on high volume exceeding the price of the previous rally and a reaction down to the previous bottom on light volume. The right shoulder is composed of a rally up that fails to exceed the height of the head. It is then followed by a reaction down. This last reaction down should break a horizontal line drawn along the bottoms of the previous lows from the left shoulder and head. This is the point at which the major decline begins. The major difference between a head and shoulder top and bottom is that the bottom should have a large burst of activity on the breakout.

Hedging—A means of protection against extensive loss due to adverse price fluctuations. In the futures market, to purchase or sell for future delivery as a temporary substitute for a merchandising transaction to be made later.

I

Interest arbitrage—The operation wherein debt instruments of one country are purchased to profit from the higher interest rate in another country. The operation is profitable only when the forward rate on the foreign currency is selling at a discount less than the premium on the interest rate.

Intermarket spread—A spread using futures contracts in one market spread against futures contracts in another market. An example would be the yen against the deutsche mark spread.

Introducing broker (IB)—A CFTC/NFA registered broker who solicits and services customer brokerage accounts but "introduces" (passes on) their orders to futures commission merchants for execution, clearing, and record keeping.

Inverted market—A futures market in which the nearer months are selling at premiums to the more distant months.

L

Last trading day—The final day under an exchange's rules during which trading may take place in a particular futures delivery month. Futures contracts outstanding at the end of the last trading day must be settled by delivery or, in the case of cash settlement, by an exchange of cash value differences.

Limit order—An order given to a broker with restrictions upon its execution, such as price and time.

Limit up/ limit down—A commodity exchange restriction on the maximum amount of movement up or down that a commodity can trade in a given day.

Liquidation—Same as offset. Any transaction that offsets or closes out a long or short position.

Liquidity—A market has liquidity when it has a high level of trading activity, allowing buying and selling with minimum price disturbance.

Local—A floor broker who usually executes trades only for his own account.

Long—To be a buyer or a person who has bought a futures contract to establish a market position and who has not yet closed this position with an offsetting sale. The opposite of being short.

Long the basis—A hedging technique that represents the purchase of a cash commodity and the sale of a futures against unsold inventory to provide protection against a price decline in the cash market.

M

Maintenance margin—A sum usually smaller than, but part of, the original margin (security deposit) that must be maintained on deposit at all times. If customer equity in any futures position drops to or under maintenance margin level, the broker must issue a call for the amount of money required to restore the customer's equity in the account to the original margin level.

Margin—A cash amount of funds that a customer must deposit with the broker for each contract as a sign of good faith in fulfilling the contract terms. It is not considered partial payment of purchase.

Margin call—A demand for additional cash funds because of adverse price movement.

Marked to market—Calculating the profit or loss on an open position using the most recent market price. Typically done by futures commission merchants to calculate margin calls or account balances.

Market if touched—An order with the floor broker that automatically becomes a market order if a trigger price is reached.

Market order—An order for immediate execution given to a broker to buy or sell at the best obtainable price.

Maximum daily price fluctuation—The maximum amount the contract price can change up or down during one trading session, as fixed by exchange rules.

Minimum price fluctuations—Smallest increment of price movement possible in trading a given contract. Varies by contract specification.

Momentum—Provides an analysis of changes in prices (as opposed to changes in price levels). Changes in the rate of ascent or descent are plotted. The momentum line is graphed positive or negative to a straight line representing time. The position of the time line is determined by price at the beginning of the momentum period. Traders use this analysis to determine overbought and oversold conditions. When a maximum positive point is reached, the market is said to be overbought and a downward reaction usually occurs. When a maximum negative point is reached, the market is said to be oversold and an upward reaction is indicated.

Moving average convergence-divergence (MACD)—A measure used to determine overbought or oversold conditions in the market. Written for stocks and stock indices, MACD can be used for commodities as well. The MACD line is the difference between the long and short exponential moving averages of the chosen item. The signal line is an exponential moving average of the MACD line. Signals are generated by analyzing the relationship of the two lines. As with RSI and stochastics, divergences between the MACD and prices may indicate an upcoming trend reversal.

Moving averages—Probably the best known, and most versatile, indicator among technical analysts. It can be used with the price of your choice (highs, closes, or whatever) and can also be applied to other indicators helping to smooth out volatility. As the name implies, the moving average is the average of a given amount of data. For example, a 14-day average of closing prices is calculated by adding the last 14 closes and dividing by 14. The result is noted on a chart. The next day the same calculations are performed, with the new result being connected (using a solid or dotted line) to yesterday's, and so forth. Variations of the basic moving average are the weighted and exponential moving averages.

N

Nearbys—The nearest delivery months of a commodity futures market. Typically these are the most active contracts.

Nominal price—Price quotation in futures for a period in which no actual trading took place.

Notice day—A day on the exchange calendar when notices of intent to deliver pertaining to a specified delivery month may be issued.

O

Offer—Indicates a willingness to sell a futures contract at a given price.

Omnibus account—An account carried by one futures commission merchant with another futures commission merchant in which the transactions of two or more persons are combined and carried in the name of the originating broker rather than designated separately.

On-balance volume (OBV)—One of the most popular volume indicators, developed by Joseph Granville. Constructing an OBV line is very simple: The total volume for each day is assigned a positive or negative value depending on whether prices closed higher or lower that day. A higher close results in the volume for that day to get a positive value, while a lower close results in a negative value. A running total is kept by adding or subtracting each day's volume based on the direction of the close. The direction of the OBV line is the thing to watch, not the actual volume numbers.

Open—The varying time period at the beginning of the trading session officially designated by the exchange during which all transactions are considered made "at the opening." The precise time varies with the amount of activity at the opening.

Open contracts—Contracts that have been bought or sold and are still outstanding, not having been delivered upon or offset.

Open interest—A number of open contracts. Refers to unliquidated purchases or sales, never to their combined total.

Opening price—The price (or range) recorded during the period designated by the exchange at the official opening.

Option—Contracts that give the holder the right, but not the obligation, to buy or sell the underlying instrument. Option contracts are issued for individual equities, futures contracts, and indices.

Original margin—The margin needed to cover a new position.

Overbought—A market that has had a sharp decline. Rank-and-file traders (who were bullish and long earlier) have turned bearish.

Oversold—A market that has had a sharp upturn. Rank-and-file traders (who were bearish and short earlier) have turned bullish.

Over-the-counter (OTC) market—The market in which custom-tailored contracts are bought and sold between counterparties and not exchange-traded.

P

Par—The standard delivery point or points, or the quality specifications of the commodity represented in the contract. Serves as a benchmark upon which to base discounts and premiums for varying quality.

Parity—Par rate.

Point—The minimum unit in which futures prices may be expressed, e.g., 1/10 of a cent per ounce for silver.

Point and figure chart—A chart that plots price only. X's are placed in boxes representing up days; and O's are placed in boxes representing down days. There is no provision for time in point and figure charting. As long as the trend remains the same, the X's or O's are placed above or below each other. When a reversal takes place, the next vertical column starts the next trend.

Position—A person's interest in the market, either long or short, in the form of open contracts.

Position limit—The maximum number of contracts, as prescribed by an exchange or the CFTC, either net long or net short, in one commodity or in all futures of the commodity combined that may be held or controlled by one person or firm in its own name. Does not apply to bona fide hedgers.

Premium—Above par. Used to quote one price in reference to another. In foreign exchange, above spot. If the forward rate for Italian lira is at a premium to spot lira, it is selling above the spot price.

Prime rate—The interest rate charged by banks to their biggest and most creditworthy customers. Other interest rates are scaled up from the prime rate, It is a good indication of general interest rate levels within a country.

Purchase and sale statement (P&S)—A statement issued by the broker to the customer showing the change in his or her net ledger balance after the offset of a previously established position.

Put—An option giving the right to sell a commodity or security at a predetermined price within a specified period of time.

Pyramiding—Using profits in a previously established position as margin for adding to that position.

R

Rally—An upward movement of prices following a decline.

Range—The high and low prices recorded during a specified time.

Rate of change—A measure used to monitor momentum by making direct comparisons between current and past prices on a continual basis. The results can be used to determine the strength of price trends. *Note*: This measure is the same as momentum except that momentum uses subtraction in its calculations while rate of change uses division. The resulting lines of these two measures operated over the same data will look exactly the same—only the scale values will differ.

Recovery—Usually describes a price advance following a decline.

Relative strength index (RSI)—This indicator was developed by Welles Wilder, Jr. Relative strength is often used to identify price tops and bottoms by keying on specific levels (usually 30 and 70) on the RSI chart, which is scaled from 0 to 100. The study is also useful to detect the following:

1. Movement that might not be as readily apparent on the bar chart.
2. Failure swings above 70 or below 30 which can warn of coming reversal.
3. Support and resistance levels.
4. Divergence between the RSI and price, which is often a useful reversal indicator.

The relative strength index requires a certain amount of lead-up time in order to operate successfully.

Round turn—The purchase and sale of a contract. The long or short position of an individual is offset by an opposite transaction or by accepting or making delivery of the actual commodity.

S

Scalp—To trade for small gains. Involves establishing and liquidating a position quickly, within the same day, hour, or minute.

Security deposit—The amount of funds that must be deposited by a customer with his or her broker for each futures contract as a guarantee of fulfillment of the contract. It is not considered part payment of purchase. Used interchangeably with "margin."

Security deposit call—A demand for additional cash funds because of adverse price movement.

Settlement price—The dally price at which the clearinghouse clears all trades and settles all accounts between clearing members for each contract month. Settlement prices are used to determine both margin calls and invoice prices for deliveries.

Short—To be a seller or a person who has sold a futures contract to establish a market position and who has not yet closed out his or her position through an offsetting purchase or delivery. The opposite of being long.

Short selling—Selling a contract with the idea of buying it back at a later date.

Short squeeze—A situation in which a lack of supplies tends to force those who have sold to cover their positions by offsetting them in the futures market rather than by delivery,

Short the basis—The forward sale of a cash commodity hedged by the purchase of a futures against the cash position.

Speculator—A person who attempts to anticipate price changes and through market activities to make profits.

Spot—A market of immediate delivery of the product and immediate payment. Also refers to the nearest delivery month on a futures contract.

Spread—(1) The difference in the prices of a currency between various future deliveries or between the spot market and a future delivery. (2) To take a simultaneous long and short position, aimed at a profit via fluctuation of a differential in two prices. Also referred to as a "straddle."

Stochastics—The stochastic indicator is based on the observation that as prices increase, closing prices tend to accumulate ever closer to the highs for the period. Conversely, as prices decrease, closing prices tend to accumulate ever closer to the lows for the period. Trading decisions are made with respect to divergence between %D (one of the two lines generated by the study) and the item's price. For example, when a commodity or stock makes a high, reacts, and subsequently moves to a higher high while corresponding peaks on the %D line make a high and then a lower high, a bearish divergence is indicated. When a commodity or stock has established a new low, reacts, and moves to a lower low while the corresponding low points on the %D line make a low and then a higher low, a bullish divergence is indicated. Traders act upon this divergence when the other line generated by the study (K) crosses on the right-hand side of the peak of the %D line in the case of a top, or on the right-hand side of the low point of the %D line in the case of a bottom. Two variations of the stochastic indicator are in use: regular and slow. When the regular plot of the stochastic is too choppy, the slow version can often clarify the results by reducing the sensitivity of the calculations. The formula is

$$\%K = 100[(C - L5)/(H5 - L5)]$$

Note: Five days is the most commonly used value for %K. The %D line is a 3-day smoothed version of the %K line:

$$\%D = 100(H3/L3)$$

where $H3$ is the 3-day sum of $(C - L5)$ and $L3$ is the 3-day sum of $(H5 - L5)$.

Stoller STARC bands—In a conference held in Tokyo in spring 1990, Manning Stoller presented a technique called STARC bands. STARC bands consist of a channel surrounding a simple moving average. In STARC bands, average true range is used as a volatility measure. The width of the created channel varies with a period of the average range; thus the name ("ST" for Stoller, plus "ARC" for Average Range Channel). Like Bollinger bands, these bands will tighten in low volatility markets and widen when volatility increases. However, rather than being based on closing process, the STARC bands are based on the average true range, thus giving a more detailed picture of the market volatility. STARC bands define upper and lower limits for a normal price action, whereas the penetration of a Bollinger band may indicate a continuation of a price move.

Stop loss order—An order that immediately becomes a market order when the "stop" level is reached. Its purpose is to limit losses. It may be implemented either by buying an order or by selling an order.

Straddle—In futures trading, the same as the spread. Straddles (spreads) are between delivery months.

Swap—An interest rate swap is an agreement between two parties to exchange interest rate payments on a fixed (notional) amount of debt. In its standard (generic) form, one party to the swap agrees to pay a fixed interest rate in exchange for receiving a variable (floating) rate on the swap's notional amount. The reverse position is taken by the counterparty. Typically, the floating-rate side of the swap is tied to the 3- or 6-month LIBOR (London interbank offer rate). In foreign exchange, an exchange of bank balances.

Switching—Liquidating an existing position and simultaneously reinstating that position in another contract month of the same commodity or currency.

T

Technical rally—A price movement attributed to conditions developing from within the futures market itself. These conditions include changes in open interest, volume, and extent of recent price movement.

Tick—Refers to a minimum change in price.

Treasury bills—Government debt obligations. They are sold at something less than their value at maturity, the difference thereby being the yield. For example, a 1-year U.S. Treasury bill worth $10,000 at maturity may sell at $9600. The $400 difference would be the yield, which is 4.17 percent (400/$9600).

Trend—The general direction of the market.

V

Volatility—The degree to which the price of a stock or futures contract tends to fluctuate over time. Volatility measures the speed of price moves. A slow-moving market has low volatility; a fast-moving market has high volatility. Additionally, options for the sale or purchase of futures contracts and stocks are also traded at an agreed price in the market through supply and demand. Volatility is important in determining the price of options as well as being used in several technical techniques to predict market behavior.

Based on an option's market price, we can calculate back the volatility, which is referred to as "implied volatility" or "market expected volatility." The values for all the inputs except volatility are easily obtained. To arrive at a volatility there are two methods employed: implied volatilities from the price of an option and tracking the actual historical volatility from the underlying issue. These statistically expected futures ranges, in various time periods, are expressed in futures points. For example, if the 1-week standard deviation is 1.52 and the current futures price is 55.00, then statistically there is a 68.3 percent chance that within a 7-day time period, the futures will range between 53.48 and 56.52. Two times the standard deviation (3.04 futures points) represents a 95.4 percent statistical chance, and three times (5.56 futures points) represents 99.7 percent.

Volatility is the most basic statistical risk measure. It can be used to measure the market risk of a single instrument or an entire portfolio of instruments. While volatility can be expressed in different ways, the standard definition for volatility which is used in finance is: The volatility of a random variable is the standard deviation of its return.

For example, the S&P 500 has annual volatility of about 15 percent. Intuitively, this might be interpreted as meaning that, over a typical year, the value of the stock market will stray from its anticipated year-end value by about 15 percent.

While implied volatilities are useful in certain applications, they can be calculated only if there is a liquid market for a corresponding option. For example, implied volatilities can be calculated for many currencies or for the S&P 500; whereas they cannot be calculated for most municipal bonds of the portfolio of a pension plan. For this reason, implied volatilities can be of limited usefulness to risk managers.

Volume—The number of purchases or sales of a commodity futures contract made during a specified period of time.

Volume accumulation—This volume indicator addresses some of the on-balance volume's shortcomings and was developed by Marc Chaikin. Where OBV assigns all of a day's volume a positive or negative value, volume accumulation counts only a percentage of the volume as positive or negative, depending on where the close is in relation to the average price of the day. The only time the entire day's volume is assigned a positive value is when the close is the same as the day's high. The opposite applies for a close at the day's low.

Index

Action plans, 36
Alliances, 175
Analysis, trade, 70
APIs, standardized, 154
Arbitrage with E-minis,
    178–180
Arbor, Pat, 21
AuditTrack concept, 166

Back-office platforms,
    159–160
Bands:
    for momentum indicators,
        88
    for moving averages,
        108–109
Bandwidth, 152–153
Basic credit controls,
    172–174
Beanie Babies, 44–45
Benchmarks for goals, 35

Bifurcated markets, 29–30
Black box systems, 63
Breakout filters, 109
Brennen, David, 21
Broadband technology, 148
BrokerTec, 164–165
Bulletin board technology,
    147–148

Cable modems, 150–151
Cantor Fitzgerald, 22, 191
Capital for margin, 136
Capitalism, 200–201
Casino gambling, 41
Catania, Patrick, interview
    with, 156–169
CFTC (Commodity Futures
    Trading Commission), 30
Chalkboards, 5–6
Changes:
    fear of, 145–146

Changes (*Cont.*):
  in portfolio management,
    71–72
Chicago Board of Trade:
  membership in, 168
  need for, 164–165
  position shifts by, 157–159
  restructuring plans by, 162
Circuit breakers, 156,
  173–174
Clearing firms, 10, 173
Commissions, 42
Commitment-of-traders
  reports, 126–127
Commodity Futures Trading
  Commission (CFTC), 30
Communism, failure of, 200
Compatibility in upgrades,
  143
Competition, 154
Compulsive gambling, 43–44
Consolidation periods:
  open interest in, 126
  stochastics for, 91
Contract liquidity, 138–139
Cooperation from
  demutualization,
  162–163
Core indicators, 75
  momentum, 79–88
  oscillators, 76–79
  relative strength index,
    97–101
  stochastics, 88–94
Corn contracts, 167
Costs:
  and competitiveness, 158
  of memberships, 163–164
  of open-outcry-electronic
    system integration,
    159–160

Costs (*Cont.*):
  startup, 142–143
Credit cards, 146
Credit controls, 172–174
Critical thinking, 60
Crossover method, 85
Crowd psychology, 180–181
CUBS (Universal Broker
  Station), 15
Currencies:
  importance of, 8–9
  for trending, 130–131
Customers:
  demands by, 152
  European vs. US, 163–164
  resistance by, 145–146

Dangers and opportunities,
  193–194
Deadlines for high-E people,
  59
Delayed signals with
  percentage filters, 110
Delegated market makers, 155
Demutualization:
  benefits of, 162–163
  importance of, 200–202
Dial-up modem technology:
  introduction of, 147–148
  limitations of, 12
  speed of, 150–151
Discipline, 37–38, 139
Discussion groups, 64
Diversification, 134–136
Dollar units for margins,
  137–138
Double-crossover method,
  110–111
Downtrends, open interest
  in, 125
Dummy alerts, 173–174

E-minis:
  advantages and
    disadvantages of,
    178–179
  arbitrage with, 178–180
  introduction of, 16–17,
    22–23, 177–178
  liquidity with, 155, 172–174
EFPs (exchange for
    physicals), 170–171
Electronic communications
    networks (ECNs), 30
Electronic standardization,
    153–154
Emotion:
  in even tendency people,
    65–66
  high-E success approach,
    57–59
  high-E tendencies, 56–57
  vs. intellect, 51–56
  summary, 205–207
  in trading from home, 181
Eurex platform:
  evaluation of, 188–189
  integration with, 169
  and open outcry, 160–161
Eurodollars, 176, 192
Evaluating goals, 36
Even tendency people, 65–66
Exchange floors, closing of,
    155–156
Exchange for physicals
    (EFPs), 170–171
Exiting position:
  procedures for, 135
  timing of, 72–73

Fads, 44–45
Fail safes, 172–173
Fair trade policies, 174

False signals, 81
Fast stochastics, 91
Fear factors, 145–146
Federal regulatory issues,
    165–166
Filters for moving averages,
    105, 108–110
Financial Industry Exchange
    (FIX), 20
Five-step plan, 67–69
  analyzing trades, 70
  exiting position, 72–73
  identifying profitable
    trades, 69–70
  managing portfolio for
    change, 71–72
  minimizing risk and
    maximizing reward,
    71
FIX (Financial Industry
    Exchange), 20
Foreign currencies:
  importance of, 8–9
  for trending, 130–131
14-day RSIs, 98
Free markets, 200–201
Future of electronics, 25–31,
    195–196
Futures and derivatives
    exchanges list,
    209–223

Gambling:
  and impulsive behavior,
    43–44
  psychological indicators,
    39–43
Geography, irrelevance of,
    198–199
Globalization, 201–202
Globex systems, 16, 170–176

Goals, 33–34
  discipline for, 37–38
  setting, 35–37
Government actions:
  consistency in, 130–131
  price controls, 7–8
  regulatory issues, 165–166
Grain contracts, 167
Groups:
  behavior in, 46–48
  for high-E people, 58–59
  for high-I people, 64

Hackers, 146
Help groups, 46
High bands for moving
  averages, 108–109
High-volume blow-off,
  123–124
Homes, trading from,
  180–181

IBs (introducing brokers),
  10–11
Impulsive behavior, 43–44
Indicators, 75
  momentum, 79–88
  oscillators, 76–79
  relative strength index,
    97–101
  stochastics, 88–94
Inflation and interest rates,
  130
Information and technology
  age, 131
Innovation, ramifications of,
  194
Intellect:
  vs. emotion, 51–56
  in even tendency people,
    65–66

Intellect (*Cont.*):
  high-I success approach,
    62–65
  high-I tendencies, 60–62
Interest rates for trending,
  130
Interfaces, standardized, 154
International Petroleum
  Exchange (IPE), 175
Internet:
  initial response to, 13–15
  resistance to, 142, 144–145
Interviews:
  Catania, Patrick, 156–169
  Melamed, Leo, 183–194
  Rand, John, 176–183
  Sander, Jack, 194–204
  Serpico, Donald, 170–176
  Starnes, Charles, 152–156
  Susz, Glen, 142–151
Introducing brokers (IBs),
  10–11
IPE (International Petroleum
  Exchange), 175

Kaiser, Bill, 6, 13
Key reversals, 123–124
Klemen, Steve, 11

Lagging indicators:
  vs. leading, 67–68
  moving averages as, 104
  oscillators as, 79
Large traders in commitment-
  of-traders reports,
  126–127
Law of unintended
  consequences, 52
Leading indicators:
  vs. lagging, 67–68
  volume as, 123

LEO (Linnco's electronic order entry system), 11–14
Leverage with margin, 136
LIFFE (London International Financial Futures Exchange), 175
Linearly weighted moving averages, 105
Linnco Futures Group, 11
Liquidity:
  circuit breakers for, 156
  contract, 138–139
  with E-minis, 155, 172–174
  in electronic trading, 29
  with local traders, 155, 196–199
Locals, liquidity with, 155, 196–199
London International Financial Futures Exchange (LIFFE), 175
Long bonds, changes in, 162
Long-term indicators, 70
Longer-term moving averages, 104
Low bands:
  for momentum indicators, 88
  for moving averages, 108–109

Magnet effect, 190–191
Malls, shopping, 190–191
Margins:
  dollar units for, 137–138
  requirements for, 136–137
Market makers, 155
Mass behavior, 46–48
MATIF exchange, 19–20
Maximizing reward, 71

Meat markets, 129–130
Media-induced opinions, 48–49
Melamed, Leo, interview with, 183–194
Membership seats:
  in CBOT, 168
  costs of, 163–164
  value of, 20–21, 198–199
Mental conditioning, 53
Minimizing risk, 71
Modem technology:
  introduction of, 147–148
  limitations of, 12
  speed of, 150–151
Momentum indicators, 79–88
Money management techniques:
  contract liquidity, 138–139
  diversification, 134–136
  dollar units for margins, 137–138
  margin requirements, 136–137
  self-discipline, 139
Money supply policies, 131
MOS (mutual offset system), 20
Moving averages, 103–107
  double-crossover method, 110–111
  filters for, 105, 108–110
  high and low bands for, 108–109
  percentage bands for, 108
  rubber band theory for, 116
  for trend identification, 69–70
  triple-crossover method, 111, 116

Mutual offset system (MOS), 20

National Futures Association (NFA), 30–31
Never enough indicator syndrome, 206
New York Cotton Exchange, 22
New York Mercantile Exchange, 175
News, creating, 49
NFA (National Futures Association), 30–31
9-day RSIs, 98

One-contract approach for stochastics, 96–97
Open interest, 117–119
   commitment-of-traders reports for, 126–127
   interpreting, 124–126
Open-outcry system:
   benefits of, 158
   electronic system integration costs with, 159–160
   for options, 188
Opportunities and dangers, 193–194
Options, open-outcry system for, 188
Original stochastics, 91
Oscillators, 76–79
Outlook for electronic trading, 25–31, 195–196

Palm PDA operating system, 31
Participation in high-I people, 62

PDAs (personal data assistants), 31
Pearl Harbor complex, 47–48
Penney, J. C., 33
Percentage bands for moving averages, 108
Percentage filters for moving averages, 110
Personal data assistants (PDAs), 31
Plans, 36
   analyzing trades, 70
   exiting position, 72–73
   identifying profitable trades, 69–70
   managing portfolio for change, 71–72
   minimizing risk and maximizing reward, 71
Playing field for individual investors, 181–182
Positive outcome expectations, 41–42
Price controls, 7–8
Priorities for high-E people, 59
Product features, importance of, 175
Product testing, 189–190
Profit potential, identifying trades with, 69–70
Proprietary products, 192
Psychological indicators:
   fads and speculative bubbles, 44–45
   gambling, 39–42
   group behavior, 46–48
   impulsive behavior, 43–44
   media-induced opinions, 48–49
   summary, 205–207

Psychology of the crowd, 180–181
Public acceptance of technology, 151
Public accessibility, 167

Rand, John, interview with, 176–183
Rate changes with momentum indicators, 85
Raw stochastics, 91–94
Regulatory issues:
  bifurcated markets, 30
  electronic trading, 165–166
Relative strength index (RSI), 97–101
Research reports, 149–150
Resistance:
  determining level of, 133–134
  from establishment, 185–187
  to Internet, 142, 144–145
Restating and refining goals, 36
Restructuring plans by CBOT, 162
Retail accounts:
  future of, 26
  increases in, 166–167
Risk:
  managing, 201–202
  minimizing, 71
  in non-brokered trades, 147
  and self-discipline, 139
  in trading from home, 182
Risk-reward ratio, 71
Roadblocks, 142
RSI (Relative strength index), 97–101

RSI price divergencies, 99–100
RSI Reversals, 99–100
Rubber band theory, 116

Sander, Jack, interview with, 194–204
Satellite technology, 147–148
SBF (Société des Bourse Français), 19–20
Scrapbooks, 6
Seasonal cycles, open interest for, 122
Security issues, 145–146
Self-discipline, 139
Serpico, Donald, interview with, 170–176
Shopping malls, magnet effect in, 190–191
Shorter-term moving averages, 104
Side-by-side trading, 23
Signal strength in stochastics, 96–97
SIMEX (Singapore International Monetary Exchange), 20, 185
Smoothing:
  moving averages for, 104
  stochastics, 94
Socialism, failure of, 200
Société des Bourse Français (SBF), 19–20
Software costs, 143
Speculation, benefits of, 201
Speculative bubbles, 44–45
Speed, importance of, 150–151
Spending patterns, 132
Standardization, electronic, 153–154

Starnes, Charles, interview
with, 152–156
Startup costs, 142–143
Stochastics, 88–94
signal strength in,
96–97
three-contract approach
for, 95–96
Stock market for trending,
130–132
Subjective control in high-I
people, 62
Supply-demand curves,
129–130
Support groups, 46
Support levels, 133–134
Susz, Glen, interview with,
142–151
Systematic analysis, 70

Technology:
changes in, 147–148
fear of, 145–146
limitations of, 171–172
Telegraphs, 5
Telephones, 5
10-day momentum
indicators, 81–85
Terms, glossary of,
225–249
Three-contract approach for
stochastics, 95–96
Tier levels, 187–190
Timber Hill, 177
Time filters for moving
averages, 108
Time frames for refining
goals, 36
Timing:
of exiting position, 72–73
purchases, 71

TOPS (Trade Order
Processing System):
development of, 9–10
link with Globex, 16
operation of, 13
popularity of, 23
Total-range filters, 109
Tracking goal progress, 36
Trademarks, 192
Trades:
with profit potential,
identifying, 69–70
systematic analysis of, 70
Trading cards, 6
Trading engine requirements,
175–176
Trading signals:
for even tendency people,
66
for high-I people, 62–63
with momentum
indicators, 85
in stochastics, 96–97
Transitions, preparing for,
195–196
Trending groups, 129–130
Trending markets:
moving averages in, 104
oscillators in, 76–79
stock market as, 131–132
Trends:
currencies for, 130–131
profit potential from,
69–70
stochastics for, 91
Triple-crossover method,
111, 116

Unintended consequences,
law of, 52
Upgrades, cost of, 143

Upper bands with
  momentum indicators, 88
Uptrends, open interest in,
  124–125

Video technology, 148
Volume:
  explanation of, 117–118
  interpreting, 122–124

WATER goal setting process,
  35–37
Weather product, 174–175
Web sites, resistance to, 142
Weighted moving averages,
  105

Weinberg, Max, 4
Wilder, J. Welles, 97
Windows operating system,
  resistance to, 145
Windows CE operating
  system, 31
Wireless technology, 148
Writing down goals,
  35–36

ZAP Futures Division:
  goals of, 33–34
  Internet product by, 14
  satellite system by, 12
ZAP order entry system,
  14, 180

About the Authors

WILLIAM S. KAISER is president, co-founder, and a managing director of ZAP Futures, the oldest and largest online futures brokerage firm and a division of Refco. Kaiser started his career as a runner at the Chicago Mercantile Exchange in 1968. He and his firm have been featured in *Futures*, *Bridge Trader*, *Business Week*, the *Wall Street Journal*, the *Chicago Tribune*, and on CNBC.

JAMES E. GREEN, PH.D., J.D., is general counsel, co-founder, and a managing director of ZAP Futures.